CALIFORNIA
FROM THE AIR

The Golden Coast

CALIFORNIA FROM THE AIR

The Golden Coast

Photography by BARON WOLMAN

Text by RICHARD REINHARDT,
MICHAEL GOODWIN, TOM JOHNSON
and JOHN BURKS

Design by PHIL CARROLL
and GEORGIA GILLFILLAN

CHRONICLE BOOKS □ SAN FRANCISCO

10   9   8   7   6   5

First paperback edition 1984 by Chronicle Books
Published by arrangement with Squarebooks
A production of California One Limited

Copyright © 1981 by Squarebooks, Inc.

Photographs copyright 1981 by Baron Wolman

Composition: Hansen & Associates
Production assistants: Zand Gee and Jim Wiseman

ISBN: 0-87701-320-9

Chronicle Books
San Francisco, CA 94102

Library of Congress Cataloging in Publication Data

Wolman, Baron.
   California from the air.

   1. California—Aerial photographs   2. California—
Description and travel—1981   Views. I. Reinhardt,
Richard.   II. Title.
F862.W84 1984   917.94   84-3160

Printed in Hong Kong by South Sea Int'l Press Ltd.

*I do not know what I may appear to the
world; but to myself I seem to have been only like a boy playing
on the seashore, and diverting myself in now and then
finding a smoother pebble or a prettier shell than ordinary,
whilst the great ocean of truth lay all
undiscovered before me.*

— Sir Isaac Newton

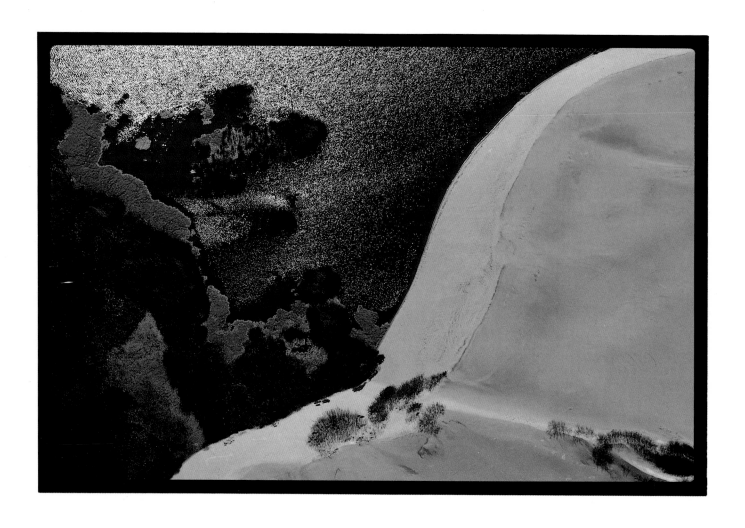

Oso Flaco Lake near Oceano, San Luis Obispo County

C O N T E N T S

ABOVE IT ALL *by Baron Wolman*   9

IN THE BEGINNING *by Richard Reinhardt*   15

UNDERWATER BIOLOGIST *Wheeler North*   29

PHOTOGRAPHER *Ansel Adams*   37

THE CONSTRUCTION OF HIGHWAY ONE *Tom Neff*   45

CALIFORNIA HIGHWAY PATROLMAN *Ken Wright*   49

NEPENTHE *Lolly & Bill Fassett*   53

THE LAST LIGHTHOUSE KEEPER *Guy C. Sheets*   57

THE COAST COMMISSIONER *Melvin Lane*   61

CITIZEN ENVIRONMENTALIST *Lenore Roberts*   71

THE GEOLOGY OF THE COAST *Kenneth Lajoie*   83

SEA RANCH ARCHITECT *Joseph Esherick*   89

BAR PILOT *Captain John Weiss*   97

SANTA MONICA CANYON & BEACH *Jon Carroll*   107

CHIEF WARRANT OFFICER, US COAST GUARD *Terry "O" Gallaher*   115

THE SURFER-OCEANOGRAPHER *George Domurat*   121

TRIBAL SPIRITUAL LEADER *Loren Bommelyn*   127

ESALEN *Michael Murphy*   131

FROM HERE TO ECOTOPIA *Ernest Callenbach*   135

THE NEPTUNE SOCIETY *Richard Jongordon*   141

THANKS . . .   143

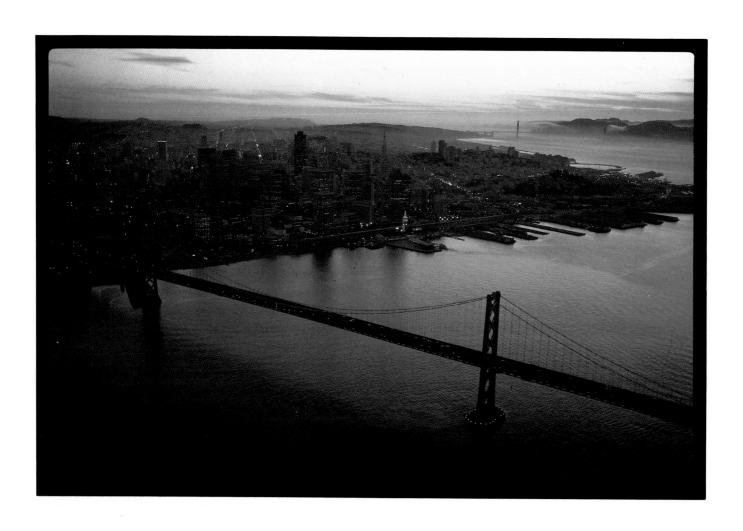

Dusk in San Francisco

A B O V E   I T   A L L

by Baron Wolman

I was born landlocked, and it bothered me. Oh sure, Alum Creek was within walking distance, and we crossed the Olentangy River in a car every Sunday on the way to the golf course where I caddied for my father. But Columbus, in central Ohio, was definitely without a serious body of water — a shortcoming of significance.

One weekend we drove up to Cleveland for a Brown's game in Lakefront Stadium. It was late fall, rainy and uncomfortably cold. Lake Erie was big all right, lots of water. But it was gray and foreboding, and still only a lake.

Another winter brought the family to Daytona Beach on the Atlantic. Water to be reckoned with. Gentle, but water by the mile, all the way to the horizon and on to foreign shores. We waded way out on the sandy bottom, the way you can on some Florida beaches. The Atlantic was friendly. The only worry was the sting of a man-of-war. After the vacation, of course, it was back to the heartland, back to the flatland in the middle.

Things did improve after high school: four years of college on the shore of Lake Michigan. My room was on the third floor overlooking the lake. Heaven. I stared at the water and watched the waves for hours on end. In the winter, though, the lake froze up toward the shore. Most of the water traffic — maybe all of it — ceased until the spring thaw. There was something unsettling about a frozen Great Lake; a real body of water didn't just freeze up and shut down.

Then I started actually hearing about the other ocean. I think it was Carol Hill who fired my curiosity about the place; she came from the West and was a fellow student and friend. Not that there was any way you could ignore the existence of the Pacific, nor of California itself. We all knew they were there. But what were they, exactly? What was going on out there across the miles of plains and up and over the Rockies, far enough away to be more of an idea than a personal reality for the less-than-adventurous. You needed a hand to make the connection. Enter Jack Kerouac and Henry Miller. With their help I was hooked. I could say I didn't know it at the time, but I'd be wrong. I knew it completely, the way you know true love.

After graduation I spent the summer in a tiny studio apartment on Nob Hill, riding cable cars, exploring San Francisco — the Co-Existence Bagel Shop featured the daytime action on upper Grant Avenue — taking pictures, writing a travel column for a paper back home but never submitting a word. Letting California into my blood; three months of sinking new roots.

I joined the Army or I would have been drafted. It was a safe decision since we were between wars. Had I thought about it, I probably would have signed up in California and done basic at Fort Ord. But I decided to go home and leave in style. "Be a good soldier, son," offered my dad when he dropped me off for the swearing in. So it was off to Fort Knox and then to Fort Benning and then to Fort Holabird, and *then* to learn German at the Army Language School high on a hill overlooking Monterey Bay, back in California. That settled it. Just imagine getting up at dawn to the sounds of barking seals, to the smell of the fog and the sea air, to a horizon shadowed with distant mountains and underlined with a thin long curve of breaking surf against the light sand beach. We had evenings and weekends free, free to climb along the rocks at Pacific Grove, free to leave footprints in the sand of the Carmel beaches, free to explore Point Lobos, free to take the train up to San Francisco or down to Los Angeles, free to lunch at Nepenthe, free to leave a postcard in Henry Miller's Big Sur mailbox (he never answered), free to become permanently addicted to California and its incredible coast.

When I returned to California from Germany — there was nowhere else to go, you understand — it was to Los Angeles. My apartment was in the middle of town but my best friend lived out at the beach in Malibu in an area that was shortly to become "the colony." It was out there I was most comfortable, so I spent a lot of time with the volleyball crowd and falling asleep to the background music of waves and surf. In town I kept changing apartments: from the flatland to halfway up a Hollywood hill, finally to the top of another. If I couldn't be along the edge of the water it was important to be up above it all.

Before I got to high school, I knew that I would be leaving Columbus. I'd pedal north on Cassady Avenue to where it crossed the mainline of the Pennsylvania Railroad. I would watch the trains come from the east and from the west, rumble on by to some exotic (I was convinced) destination. I would yearn to be aboard, simply to go somewhere else. Or I would bike still further on to Port Columbus and watch a tiny speck in the sky grow into a DC-3. I fell in love with the stewardesses (and Esther Williams) and imagined torrid love affairs with them in the faraway places to which I knew the planes flew. Columbus was only a stop along a route; it was never the town *from* which the silver bird came or *to* which it was going.

Years later, when the budget allowed for a holiday plane ride back and forth between Chicago and Columbus, my earliest fantasies were fueled. There *was* something magical about flying. The drone of the engines had a distinctly narcotic effect; not only were we high, but I was high. And the smiling, solicitous stewardesses *were* gorgeous by definition. It was special up there, above it all. No earthbound cares. No problems. A comfortable seat. Refreshments on demand. That marvelous buzz. Tiny houses, tiny people, tiny troubles. Why couldn't it be like this forever?

It could and it did and it does, but it took a long time to find the formula. Into the mix went flying lessons and later on, my own Cessna. Later, I added the final ingredient of photography. The journey from Columbus led me and my camera into the air above California, on the edge of the continent, over the sea, along the coast.

The California coast today is a mix of the natural and the man-made. The hand of nature was flawless in creating an abundance of visual delights; sadly, the hand of man has not been nearly so beneficent. Yet in the traces of the latter are found some surprisingly exhilarating treats: forms and patterns and snapshots that please the eye and tickle the mind.

This celebration of our piece of the earth is meant to reflect upon this gift nature has bestowed on us, to catch a glimmer of the shore as it is today, to honor it, to help keep it healthy. I am not alone in needing and appreciating the golden coast. Many of us are nurtured and strengthened and inspired by it. If California doesn't fall away from the mainland, and if we wisely manage our inheritance, many more wanderings will end in fulfillment here in this special place. □

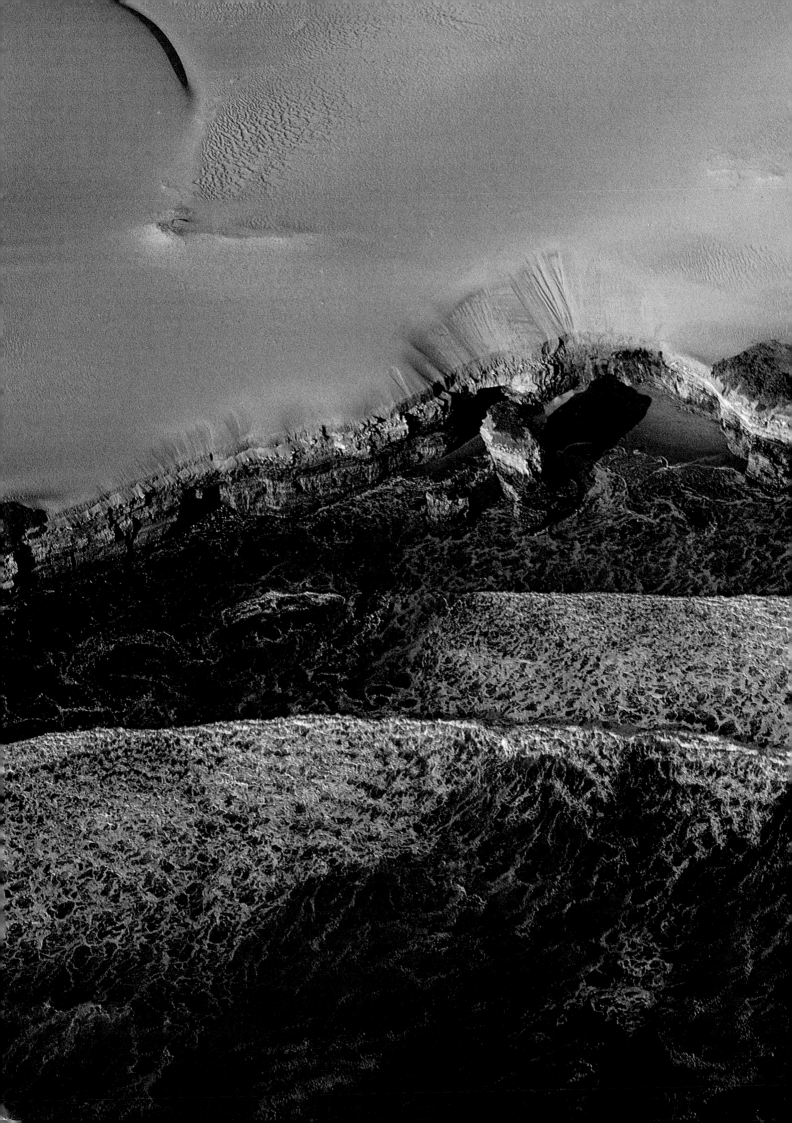

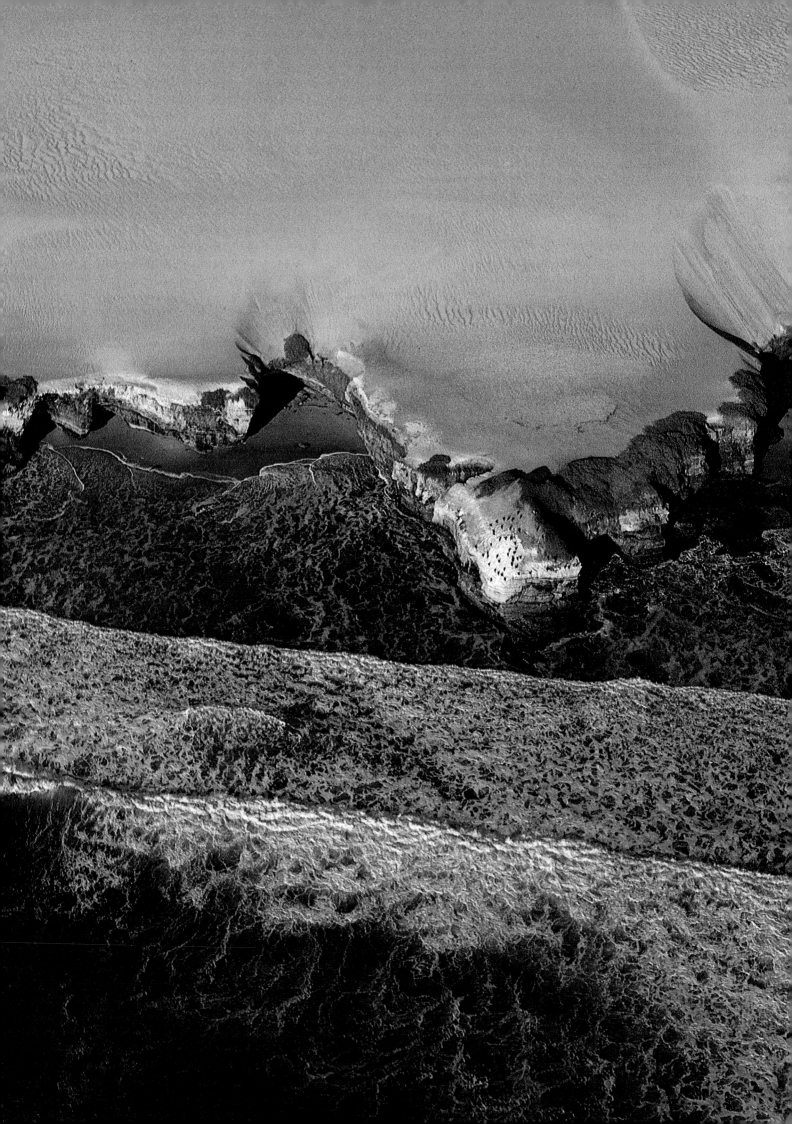

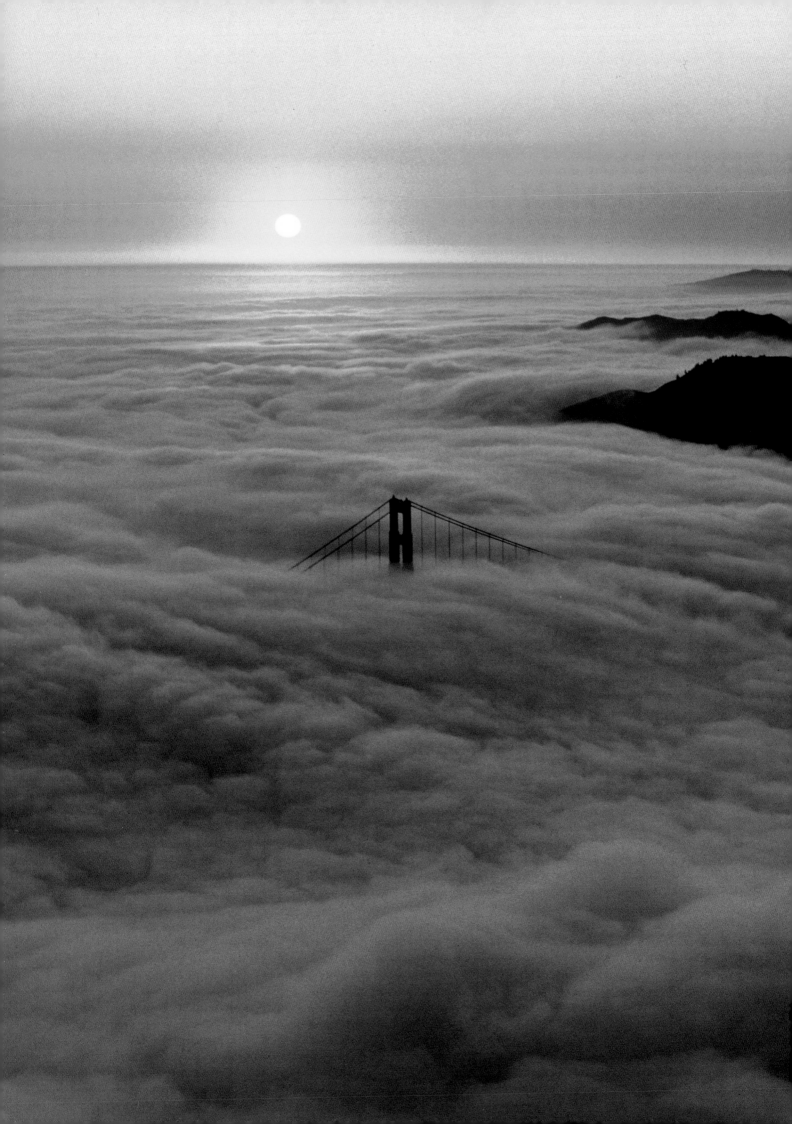

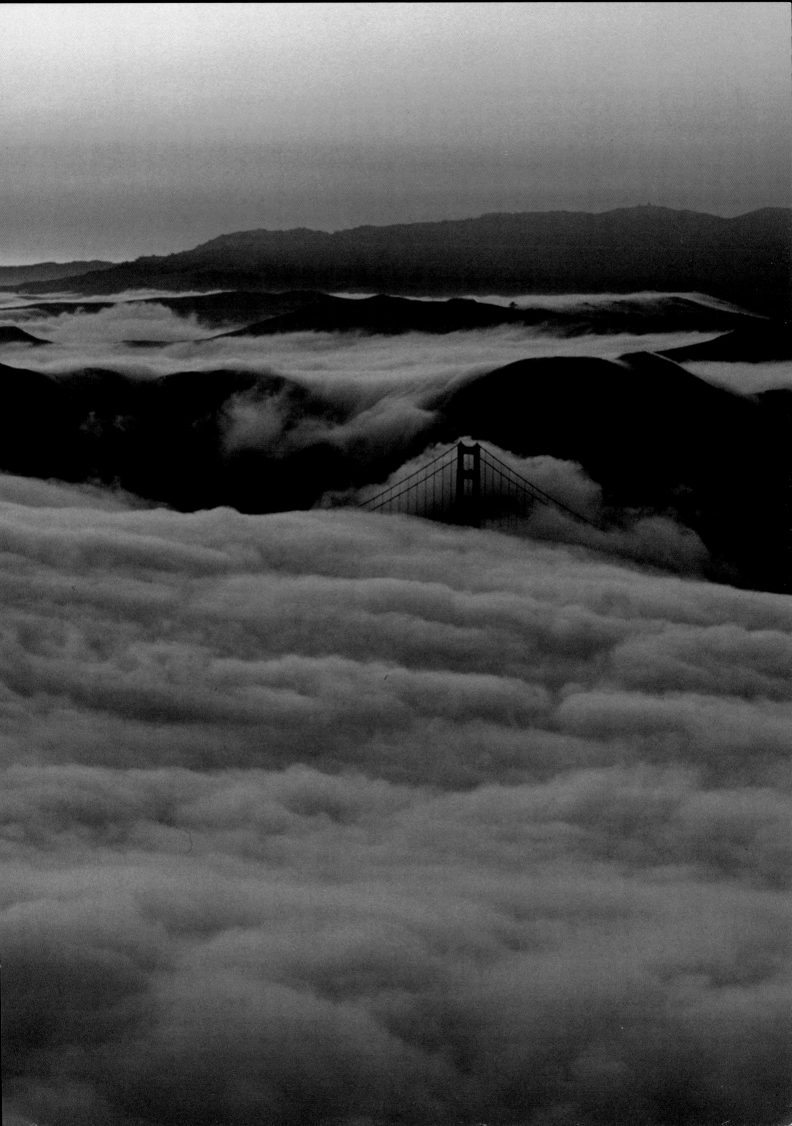

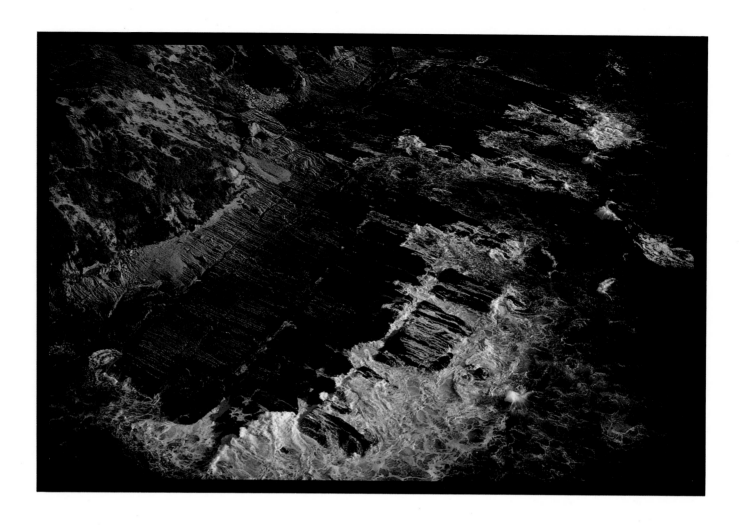

Near Point Buchon, south of Morro Bay

Pages 10 and 11: Near Purisima Point on Vandenberg Air Force Base
Pages 12 and 13: Summer fog shrouds the Golden Gate Bridge.

IN THE BEGINNING

by Richard Reinhardt

T he coast of California was created by huge, unpredictable geologic lurches and upheavals, followed by countless centuries of raising and lowering, shifting and thrashing, thrusting out and casting off, like the movements of an enormous sleeper tormented by nightmares. This twitchy shoreline, conceived with so much violence, then slumbered for thousands of years in isolation from the cries and whispers of civilization: a primitive, silent, dreaming world, without a town, without a road, without a monument, without a word of written history, inhabited by tribal people who never had heard or thought of metals, wheels, or plows, and who looked upon the ocean as a manifestation of eternity.

Discovery

Consider the peculiar manner in which the coast of California was "discovered" by Europeans — not with a breathless announcement, a casket of gold trinkets in the court of the Spanish queen or a bolt of silk unrolled in the palace of the Doge of Venice; but slowly and deliberately, through a long succession of disappointing glimpses, faulty maps, false reports, all distorted by the illusion that this forbidding shore was not the edge of a continent but only an unpleasant island upon whose shore one would not wish to be washed.

On the East Coast, the European invasion of America proceeded as if by a careful plan. Pilgrims waded ashore, uttering, "O, strange new world!" or words to that effect, and set to disciplining the local monsters and planting next year's crops. Along the California shore, few foreign visitors stayed on. Exploration was intermittent. Colonization was tardy. And when European settlers finally arrived, they were so few in number that California more resembled an outpost than a commonwealth. Ignored and misunderstood, California waited out the high season of European exploration.

The Terrain

It was a sizable piece of property to suffer such a snub The length of California from Oregon to Mexico is roughly 800 miles, and the coastline, counting all its juts and crannies, is 1,264 miles, equivalent to the Atlantic coast from Canada to Delaware. The upper end, where Cape Mendocino shoulders into the Pacific, is the most westerly place in the mainland United States, excluding Alaska. The lower end, near San Diego, is a hundred miles farther east than Reno, Nevada. Up near Mendocino, there are places where the rainfall averages 110 inches a year. In times past, the wild, brown rivers carried 200-foot redwood logs down the canyons every winter, piling them like kindling on the sand spits. Around San Diego, the rainfall averages 10 inches. The streams have di-

minutive Spanish names, and they dry up and disappear every summer.

Compared to most of the coastlines of the world, the California coast forms a relatively straight, smooth line. It runs approximately north-west to south-east. For hundreds of miles, from the Oregon border down to Santa Barbara, substantial mountains press against the shore, forming an almost unbroken barrier 2,000 to 6,000 feet high. Except for the immense flatlands of the Los Angeles basin, there are no large coastal plains; and on the entire coast there are only three natural harbors of significant size: the bays of Humboldt, San Francisco, and San Diego. Nor are there many of those useful tidal estuaries that crinkle the Atlantic coasts of Europe and North America. There are few marshes, fewer swamps, and no everglades. The only important river delta is inland, separated from the ocean by the deep lagoon of San Francisco Bay. The California shoreline typically consists of sandstone cliffs and palisades gnawed by waves and north-west winds; of step-like coastal terraces, small rocky islands, tiny wedges of sandy beach, and great, ochre-colored headlands, shrouded with summer fogs and pounded by incessant surf.

Geographers divide the coast into seven "provinces." (The State, for its own reasons, has carved these into 14 counties.)

Farthest north is the province of the Klamath, a land of jumbled mountain chains, rain forests, lumber camps. Millions of years ago, the whole region was one massive, flattish rock, forced upward by subterranean pressures and scarred deep by raging streams. Now, the Klamath, the Trinity, the Smith, and the Salmon tumble down through steep canyons. The mountains edge close to the ocean, and the only coastal plain is a narrow beachhead strewn with silver-gray driftwood. At Humboldt Bay, the Eel and the Mad Rivers form modest deltas.

Next come the corrugated, north-south ridges of the province of Northern Coastal Ranges: redwood country. Two-masted schooners used to anchor here in rockbound dog-holes during the '50s to the '80s of the last century to pick up hundreds of thousands of railroad ties and building planks. In those days there were as many as seventy-six landing places (of sorts) between Bodega Head and Humboldt Bay, each offering a mill, a lumber chute, and a promise of shelter from the wind. Three small bays also indent the coast just north of San Francisco: Bodega, where Russian fur hunters found refuge early in the 19th Century and bootleggers took delivery during Prohibition of boatloads of whiskey to be spirited away to San Francisco in undertakers' hearses; Tomales, a thin, blue finger of the sea, 12 miles long and only slightly wider than the San Andreas earthquake fault, which underlies it; and Drake's Bay, a crescent-shaped anchorage sheltered by the white cliffs of Point Reyes and named for Sir Francis the Circumnavigator, who may or may not have careened his *Golden Hinde* here in 1579.

The Golden Gate, a steep-walled channel less than a mile wide, creates the next region — the Great Gap, the only natural passage between the ocean and the interior valleys of central California. Just inside the Gate is San Francisco Bay, an inland sea ringed with cities and enclosed by hills. The two major river systems of California — the Sacramento and the San Joaquin — meet tidewater in the upper bay, and it is their estuary that forms the door to the interior. The city of San Francisco, crowning a narrow peninsula on the south side of the Gate, sometimes is described as the guardian of the straits; but, in fact, the city has always turned its back on the coast. It faces inland, gloating over its splendid harbor, its rivalrous neighbors, and its rich hinterland.

Below San Francisco is the province of the Central Coast Ranges, a continuation of the interrupted redwood country. As one goes south, the climate gradually becomes more arid. The redwoods disappear. South of Santa Cruz, the coast sweeps eastward in a crescent curve, and the mountains withdraw inland, opening the only noteworthy coastal plain in northern California — a moist, gray-green kitchen garden of artichokes and cabbages, pippin apples and loganberries. Monterey, in the southern hook of this open bay, was the Hispanic capital of Alta California. The rocky peninsula that shelters the town on the west is the touristic principality of Del Monte, Pebble Beach and Carmel, the most photographed, painted, golfed-upon, and honeymooned-at shoreline in America. Beyond Carmel lies the spectacular Big Sur, where the Santa Lucia Mountains rear up in 7000-foot peaks at the very edge of the sea.

At Point Conception, about 300 miles below San Francisco, the coast ranges veer eastward and the coast turns with them. Geographers call this the province of the Traverse Ranges. The mountains take new names: Santa Ynez, San Rafael, and Tehachapi to the north, Santa Monica, San Gabriel, and San Bernardino farther south. They run inland in great, parallel wrinkles from the coast to the Mojave Desert, marking the division between northern and southern California. The coast, too, runs almost due east from Point Conception to Santa Monica. Residents of the beach towns, with their backs against the Santa Ynez range, gaze out at a line of offshore islands that are, in fact, the peaks of another range that was swallowed 30,000 or 40,000 years ago by the rising sea.

Beyond the crumbling cliffs of Malibu, the coastline swings abruptly south while the mountains continue eastward. It is another of those rare openings between inland California and the sea — in this case, the great coastside platform known to the geographers as the Los Angeles Lowland. The coast becomes a smoothly curving line of palisades and beaches. There was no harbor here until enterprising Angelenos dredged the shallows of San Pedro to form a deep water basin that is now the major port of the Pacific Coast. This is the most urbane of coasts, an almost continuous line of apartment towers, marinas, oil fields, factories, fisheries and resorts stretching down to the borders of Mexico.

The last of the coastal provinces, called "Peninsular," was named for the similarity of its terrain to that of the Baja California peninsula, which continues south for another 800 miles. No portion of California has changed more radically in recent years. Waterless and sparsely populated through most of California's history, the San Diego area has become the second largest urban center in the state. If all the small boats moored at marinas in San Diego and Mission Bays were to put to sea in a single line, it is said they would reach from California to Hawaii. Superlatives come easily on the southern edge of the golden coast.

A Youthful Geology

The meeting of the coastal mountains — which loom so large in any description of the Pacific shore — with the ocean produces a profound influence upon the climate of California and is a major factor in the agriculture, forestry, transportation, commerce and even the history of the state. Although the granite peaks of the Sierra Nevada are better-known and better-loved, it is the gentle slopes of the coast ranges that capture life-giving rains, shelter precious vineyards and vegetable fields, and partition the landscape into its incredible variety of scenic and climatic zones.

Measured in geologic time, both the coast and its ridges are relatively young. As recently as the end of the Miocene epoch, some 13 million years ago, the shore of the Pacific lay far inland, about where the Sacramento and San Joaquin Rivers flow through the Central Valley. From the crest of the Sierra, then in early adolescence, a rough plain of volcanic debris sloped down to the shore. A line of craggy offshore islands ran parallel to the coast for hundreds of miles. These were the peaks of a subsided continent; now they are the crests of the coast range.

Late in the next epoch (the Pliocene), one of California's characteristic upheavals lifted the row of islands, forming a new mountain range that cut off the sea and created the great interior valleys. The new range eroded and sank, rose and eroded again during the next million years, meanwhile permitting the rivers to gnaw the passage now referred to as the Golden Gate. A few thousand years ago, at the close of one of the great glacial ages, the rising ocean crept back though the opening, flooded several coastal valleys and formed San Francisco Bay. A later ice age lowered the oceans and drained the bay; and a final thaw re-filled it. By that time (perhaps 10,000 years ago) human beings, who perhaps had come to North America across the Bering Straits from Asia, began to settle on the coast.

The First Inhabitants

The first inhabitants of California (like the current occupants) lived in virtually every part of the territory except the peaks above timberline. Unlike modern Californians, however, they had no particular affection for the beach. They favored the sheltered valleys, where the trees were full of acorns and the streams were full of fish — although they went to the shore to spear salmon or gather baskets of abalone, clams, and mussels. Over the centuries, their collective appetite for shellfish was prodigious. They left mounds of shells 30 feet high like seals of approval near every well-stocked oyster bed. One such mount provided enough material to pave most of the streets of Oakland.

Up on the north coast, certain tribes would venture off shore in dugout canoes fire-hollowed out of redwood logs. The Costanoans paddled around San Francisco Bay in rafts of woven reeds, and down on the Santa Barbara Channel, the Chumash put to sea in vessels made of wooden planks. But on the whole Pacific Coast, there was not a single distinctly maritime tribe. Scattered in hundreds of tiny communities, speaking 138 dialects of 21 linguistic families, the California Indians, who were perhaps 250,000 in number when the Spaniards arrived, shared a respectful reverence for the ocean. It was a place to which the spirits of the dead departed, the place where the sun retired. Some anthropologists have theorized that the Indians who put a crown of feathers on the head of Francis Drake were not suggesting kingship, as the English adventurer imagined, but were only performing customary funerary honors for these pale-faced ghosts, who seemingly had returned from the watery hereafter on the wings of a huge, white gull.

The Explorers

Drake was not the first European explorer to fight the contrary winds and currents of the California coast, although he was the first to come ashore wherever it was that he came ashore. For more than two centuries, while American history was getting started on the Atlantic Coast, Portuguese and Spanish and English captains were making desultory forays on the Pacific, setting up hand-hewn crosses, drawing fragmentary charts, sometimes leaving their bones and the timbers of their broken frigates on the uncharted rocks.

The first was a Portuguese navigator of great courage and great obscurity, whose name, Joao Rodriquez-Cabrilho, is usually Hispanicized to Cabrillo, partly in recognition that he sailed in the service of Spain, partly out of general ignorance of his painful and ill-starred journey up the west coast of Mexico and into the Bay of San Diego in 1542. Cabrilho's two small caravels were barely seaworthy and his crew of conscript sailors were weak with disease. But on he pushed to the islands of the Santa Barbara Channel, round Point Conception, and up the coast, tacking against the rowdy winds. Unable to find a safe landing, Cabrilho returned to San Miguel Island, where he died of an infection in a broken arm. His men, faithful to his orders, sailed north again until they sighted what has been identified as the south coast of Oregon. And then, having found none of the things they were looking for — a northwest passage, a city

of gold, a flock of Amazon princesses — they turned back, scurvied and starving, and caught the favorable winds to Mexico.

It was 37 years later that Drake beached his leaking, over-loaded galleon near some white cliffs at roughly 38 degrees latitude and there spent five weeks in the "stinking fog," making repairs to the vessel, observing the natives, and laying claim to the country on behalf of Queen Elizabeth. Whether the place that Drake called "New Albion" was at Drake's Estero, at Bolinas Lagoon, or inside the Golden Gate is, at this time, an irreconcilable question. Of greater importance to the history of the coast is that Drake, like the other "discoverers," went on his way.

The next important visitor — another Portuguese traveler named Sebastian Rodriguez Cermeño — did not appear for 16 years. He was enroute to Mexico with the annual galleon from Manila and orders from the viceroy to have a look at upper California; but in a storm at Drake's Bay, Cermeño lost his cargo of goodies, and it was seven years before the Spanish government was willing to authorize another exploration. This time the emissary was one Sebastian Vizcaino, a merchant with an urge to win trading concessions. His discoveries included the modest bay at Monterey, which he described with such enthusiasm that later pathfinders could not believe they were looking at the same harbor.

If this account of 60 years of brave and fumbling visits to a lonely coast appears to be perfunctory, it is because the early landings left virtually no impression on the coast of California. There remain some bits of metal, turned up by archeologists in the refuse middens of Indian settlements; some shards of Chinese porcelain from the wreckage of Cermeño's galleon; some books and maps of immense value and uncertain reliability; and a brass plaque, attributed to Drake, the authenticity of which has recently been put in doubt by metallurgical tests.

The Spanish Transformation

Nor did the reports of the explorers stimulate their royal patrons to conquer the beaches of California. When the Spanish government decided, 167 years after Vizcaino's tour, to defend its claim to upper California by planting a chain of military-missionary camps along the coast, the main column was dispatched *overland*. As feared, two support ships sailing up from the Pacific coast of Mexico ran into northwest gales. It took one of the vessels 54 days to get from San Blas to San Diego. The other — at sea for 110 days — reached California with most of her crew and passengers dead or dying.

The arrival of the "Sacred Expedition" of soldiers and missionaries in 1769 transformed California. For the next three-quarters of the century, the territory would remain inaccessible and thinly populated; but its strange isolation had ended. Within a few years, English sailors discovered that the coast swarmed with sleek, black sea otters whose pelts sold for fancy prices in Canton. Russian ships with crews of Aleut fur hunters crept down from Alaska. Massachusetts Yankees braved the storms of Cape Horn to join the fun.

In 1803, the *Lelia Byrd* of Salem put in at San Diego, defying Spanish laws against hunting and trading in the colony. On the pretext of needing supplies, the captain approached the port commander and offered him a bribe for permission to hunt otters. The port commander threw the captain in the *calabozo*, whereupon the Yankee crew stormed the jail, rescued the captain, weighed anchor and sailed away, exchanging a few parting shots with the shore battery at Point Loma. Back in New England, the captain published an article about his adventures, suggesting that it was the patriotic duty of all Americans to violate Spanish trade restrictions. The article was one of the first reports printed in the United States on the special attractions of California. While it did not set off a land rush, neither did it discourage Boston traders from poaching flagrantly in Spanish waters, nor from trafficking in otter skins with Indians, soldiers, and even missionaries. Within 40 years, the sea otters were virtually extinct; the fur seals were disappearing; and whalers from Sag Harbor and New Bedford had begun to replace the furriers as the scourge of the Pacific.

The restrictions on foreign trade relaxed in 1821, when Mexico broke away from Spain and took control of upper and lower California. San Diego and Monterey opened their ports to foreign vessels. For 25 years the coast rejoiced in the famous hide-and-tallow trade described by Richard Henry Dana in *Two Years Before the Mast*, precisely the sort of colonial milking the Spaniards would have enjoyed. Yankee sailors, carrying heavy rawhides balanced on their heads, waded out through the surf and deposited their burden of "California Banknotes" in a tossing rowboat while the ships stood two or three miles off the wicked coast. Twelve months later, they returned, selling shoes made in New England of the very hides they had bought the year before, peddling cheap combs, lace filigree, pocket mirrors and wine made in Boston. Long before the United States saw fit to annex the territory during a war with Mexico, Boston traders ruled the coast.

Annexation

Logically, the annexation began with a naval invasion: a landing party and flag-raising at Monterey, the same at Yerba Buena, followed by a few skirmishes on the inland ranchos. A regiment of volunteer soldiers from New York came around by sea to take charge of the old Spanish-Mexican presidios. They were disappointed to find the country already at peace, and cattle lowing on the beach.

Within a few years, the discovery of gold in the Sierra foothills brought ships from every nation into San Francisco Bay. The unknown coast was suddenly a cynosure. Steamers came up from Panama, loaded above the Plimsoll mark with passengers who had crossed the Isthmus on mules. Hundreds of empty barks stood on the mud of Yerba Buena Cove. Their hulls lie rotting to this day under the streets of San Francisco.

After the Gold Rush, the story of the California coast resembles that of other coasts: the building of a pier, the dredging of a channel, the opening of this or that large hotel that calls itself "The Newport of the West." These are the landmarks of a growing commonwealth, not the distinctions of a unique region. Then, too, there are the natural disasters to which most coast are prone — earthquakes, storms, slides — and the avoidable accidents, ending with a broken tanker on the shoal, a fallen plane against the coastal hills.

Plaything

As always in California, however, there is an oddity, an ironic twist. The coast that was once ignored and despised became a plaything of the world, a universal symbol of comfort, wealth, and leisure.

First the coast took on a literary dimension. The craggy peak of Point Lobos became the model for Spyglass Hill in Robert Louis Stevenson's *Treasure Island*. The ocean, itself, became a symbol of brute power in Jack London's novel *The Sea Wolf*. Walt Whitman's westering American stopped at last on California's shore, and the roar of the surf pervaded the poetry of Robinson Jeffers. Who can underrate a coast with literary value?

At the same time, there came an effluence of tourist guides and real estate promotion: "It lies there, our Mediterranean region, on a blue ocean, protected by barriers of granite from the Northern influences, an infinite variety of plain, cañon, hills, valleys, sea-coast; our New Italy without malaria, with every sort of fruit which we desire . . ." This from Charles Dudley Warner, a psalmist of Southern California in the early 1890s, strumming his lyre in praise of Coronado.

The songs began — from "California, Here I Come" to "California Dreaming." It is the beach that fuses all the images together, of an easy way of life, a freedom to do — what? To be a beach bum out in California: off-road bike, surf board, gliding on the palisades, water-skiing in the bay. Blond hair, tan skin, strong white teeth, and big, metallic music throbbing across the sand.

How can the beach of California be the paradigm of failure in *A Star is Born*? How can it also be an emblem of political opportunism in *The Ninth Wave* and a symbol of corruption in Ross MacDonald's detective fiction? Why did the coast of California, at the height of its success, become a focus of deep uneasiness about the future of such elemental necessities as sun, air, space, and water?

A Future

Traveling up and down the coast of California, seeing everywhere the works of contemporary mankind, one can easily forget that these evidences of its influence date back no farther than 200 years, and most of the conspicuous physical changes have occurred within the last 50 or 60 years.

Californians have built highways, nuclear reactors, and roller coasters at the edge of the sea. They have thrust breakwaters, yacht harbors, and artificial promontories into the deep. They have dammed streams that used to bring millions of cubic yards of sand and gravel into the Pacific every year and have raised bulkheads that interrupt the offshore flow of sand, which used to rush along like an underwater hurricane. They have flavored the ocean with sewage, garbage, pesticides, industrial chemicals, radioactive poisons, automobile carcasses; and they have devoured, destroyed, or lost track of innumerable species of fish, shell fish, birds, and marine mammals. They even have created new islands, like the tropical paradise called Rincon, a half-mile off shore between Ventura and Santa Barbara. Rincon is a platform, crowned with clumps of swaying palm trees, with an oil well in its bowels.

In 1972, in belated alarm over the accelerating tempo of development and its irreversible effects upon the coast, the State passed a law putting the future of the shore under a government-administered master plan. The measure was put on the election ballot through a citizens' petition, sponsored primarily by conservation organizations, and it was approved by the voters over the strong opposition of real estate owners and developers.

In a sense, the adoption of the coastal initiative and the advent of the California Coastal Commission brought to an end the first epoch of human influence on the California coast, a period of change from one of the most primitive to one of the most highly developed shorelines on earth. Planners and environmentalists saw the initiative as the beginning of a new era of rational land use. If the Commission achieved nothing else, it would effect a moratorium on hasty real estate development and would allow the people of the state to think about the appropriate uses of a unique resource.

The pressures on the coast continue. Demands for energy point to California's off-shore oil lands. A growing population threatens the fragile habitat of birds and animals. In 50 years these photographic images of an incomparable coast could be as quaint as the Montanus drawing, done in Amsterdam in 1671, of a throng of Miwok Indians, oblivious to the sinister future, placing a crown of feathers on the head of their first foreign visitor, the Mayor of Plymouth, Captain Francis Drake. □

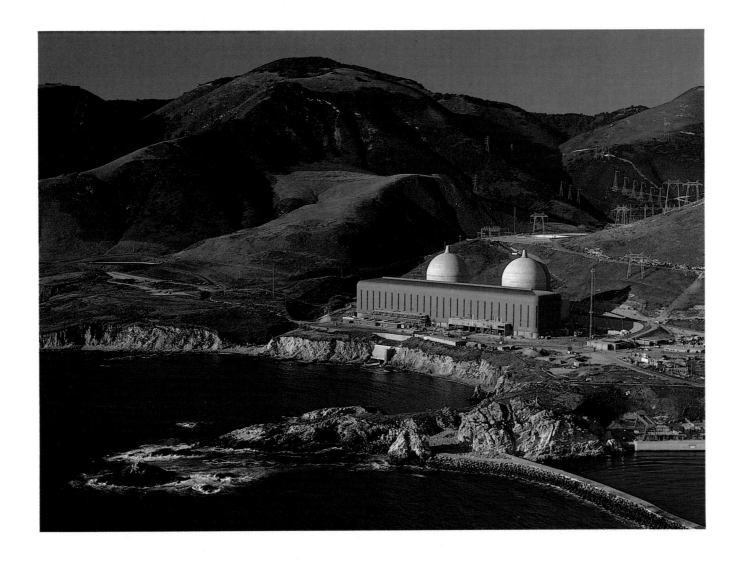

Diablo Canyon Nuclear Power Plant, San Luis Obispo County

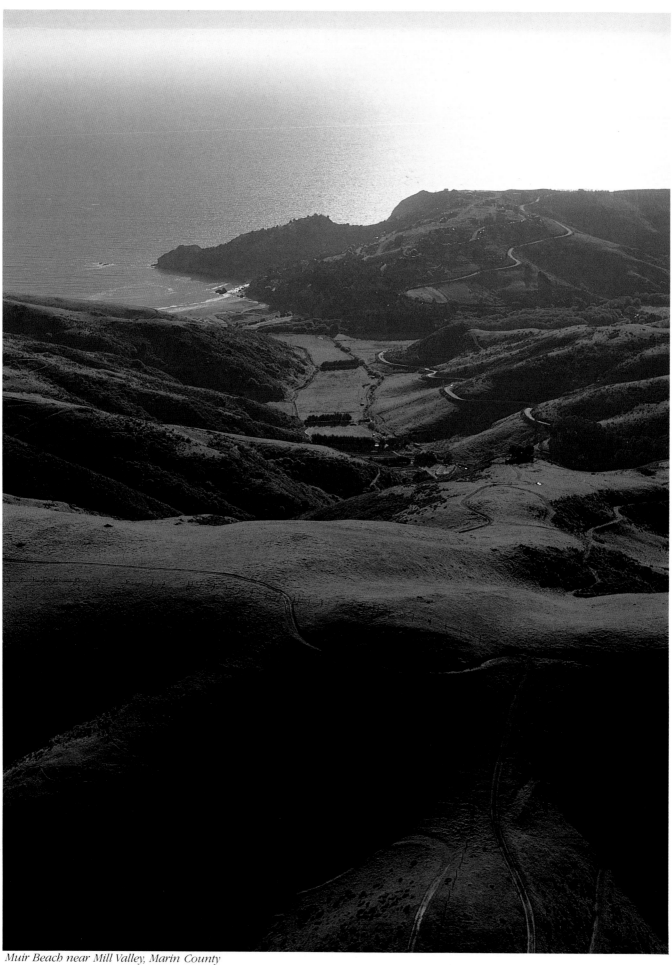

Muir Beach near Mill Valley, Marin County

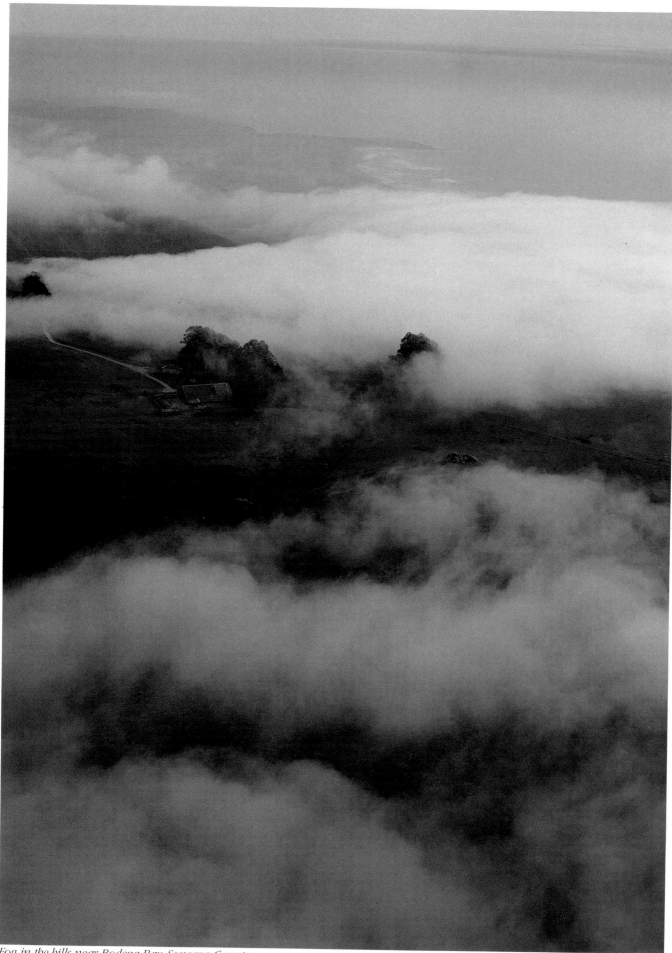

Fog in the hills near Bodega Bay, Sonoma County

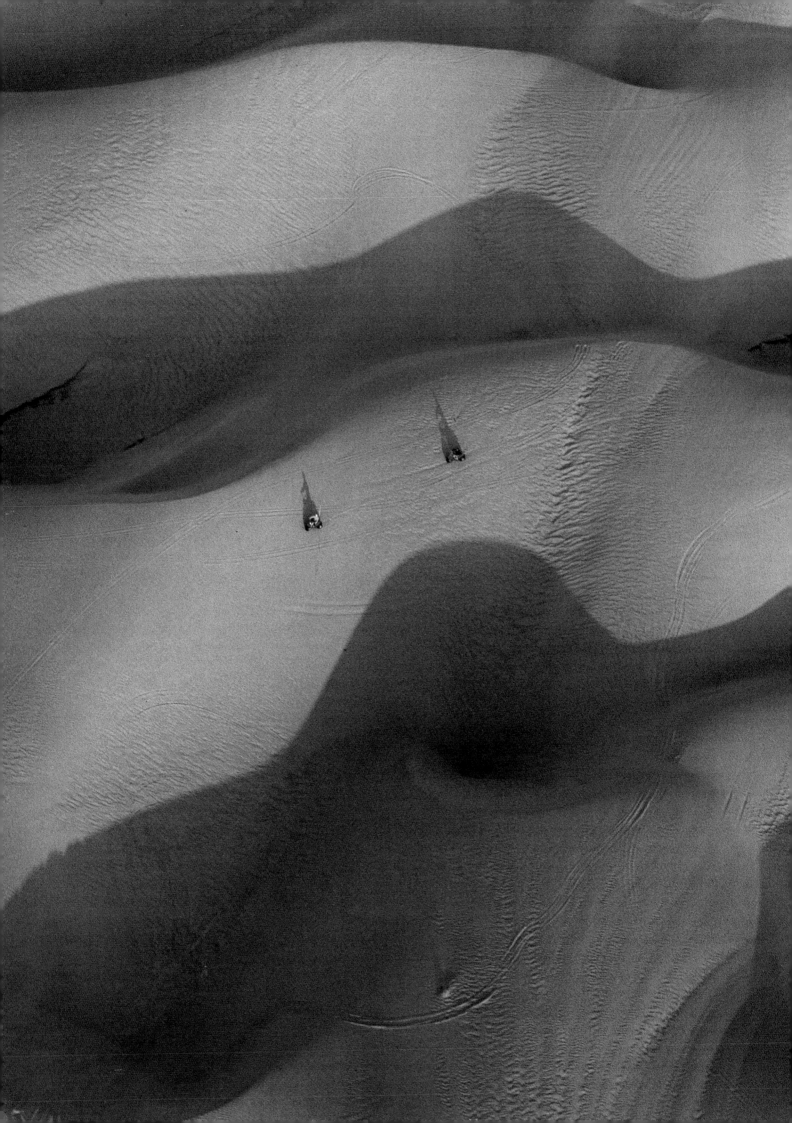

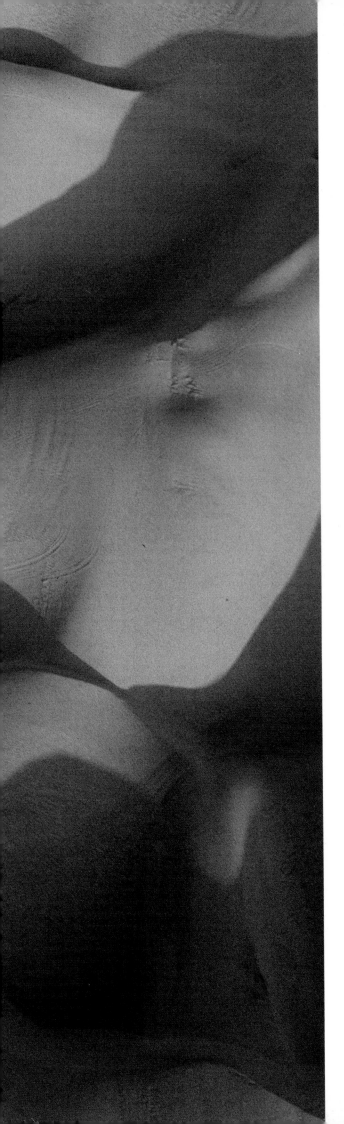

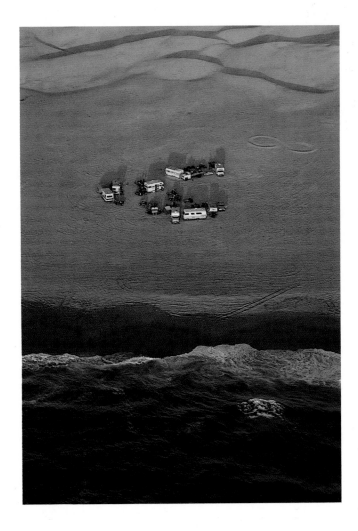

Left: Three-wheel dune cycles at the Pismo State Vehicle Recreation Area, Oceano, San Luis Obispo County

Wagon trains at the Pismo State Vehicle Recreation Area

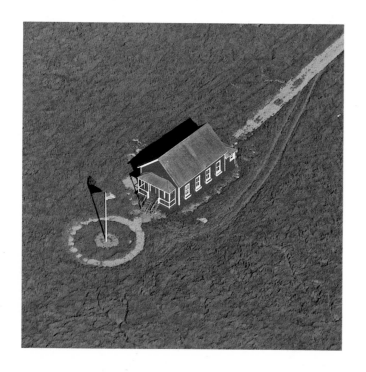

Little red schoolhouse near Orick, northern Humboldt County

Right: Morning irrigation in the Santa Maria Valley, San Luis Obispo County

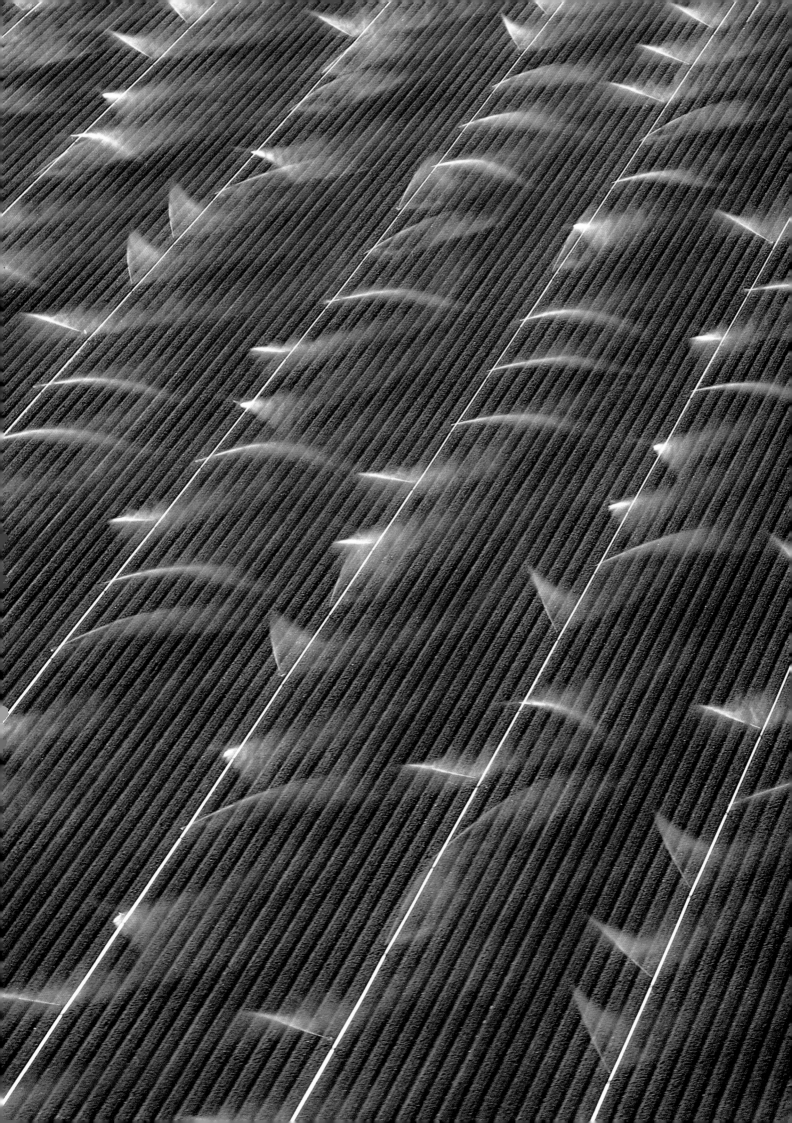

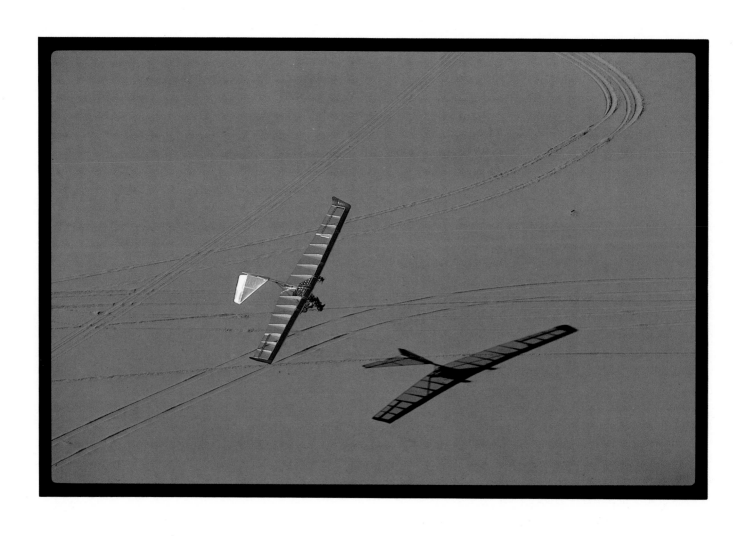

A Lazair "ultralight" over the dunes near Mussel Rock, San Luis Obispo County

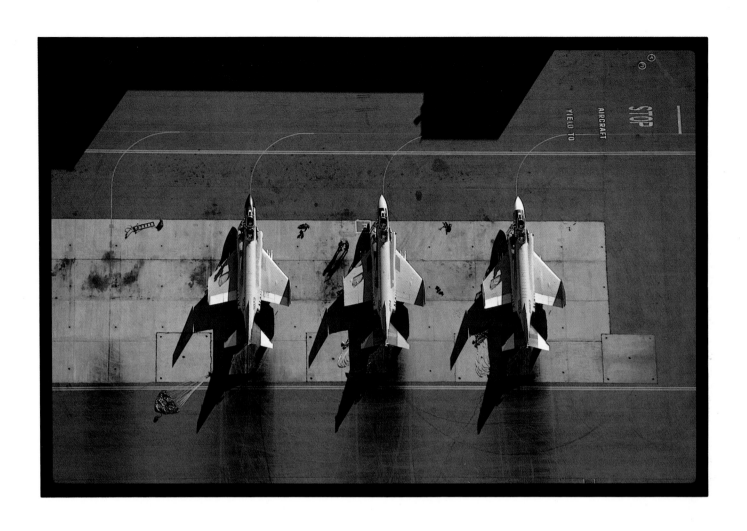

Jet fighters on the ramp at the Naval Air Station, Point Mugu in Ventura County

UNDERWATER BIOLOGIST

Wheeler North

His life moves in two quite different settings: his stuffy basement office in a concrete building at Cal Tech, in Pasadena, California; and under the waters of the California coast. He is Wheeler North, professor of environmental science, marine biologist, scuba diver, author of a book called Underwater California *(University of California Press), and after all these years he remains quietly awed by what he has found beneath the waves.*

There's a lot of variation. Some areas are deserts, and some are forests and jungles. In general, the California underwater is quite a rich area. It's intermediate between an arctic environment and a tropical environment. There are no coral reefs, but some of the loveliest areas are the kelp beds that are very well developed in places along the coast — places comparable to forests on land. Kelp happens to be my specialty, so I may be a bit prejudiced.

If you look at the California coast line there are two major boundaries that separate the underwater provinces. One boundary is at Cape Mendocino. North of that you have really rough conditions — cold water which is more or less the arctic type of climate. Coming south from there to Point Conception it's still fairly rough, but you begin to get not as severe a climate and it's very rich in plant nutrients, so you have lush vegetation. Probably the central California area is as beautiful as anything you'll find anywhere.

South of Point Conception the Channel Islands offer protection against the very large storm waves that may come in from the west. The coast slopes out more gently, so you have this long, wide shelf of relatively shallow water. You get huge kelp beds developing, because there's lots of room and protection. The water tends to be warmer, approaching the tropical — well, it's a long way from the tropical — nevertheless, you do find some tropical species in Southern California.

We also have a feature here and there called the submarine canyons, very fascinating places to dive. The Monterey Canyon that comes into Monterey, for instance, is of the same dimensions as the Grand Canyon in Arizona. It's a huge chasm. The submarine canyons have relief in them that's sometimes as spectacular as any terrestrial canyon.

The depth depends on whether you're at the head end or down at the bottom end. The La Jolla Submarine Canyon, for instance, dumps out at a depth of about 2,000 feet, too deep for any scuba diver to get to. On the edge of the La Jolla underwater canyon there's a cliff that's 700 feet high. I've found creatures in the canyons that apparently make their way up from the depths — creatures you don't usually see unless you get sophisticated oceanographic gear that can dredge down really deep. But here they're crawling up, and you find them at shallower depths than usual.

Aside from diving, and writing about it, what does your job as a marine biologist and environmental scientist involve?

A good deal of my work has focused on restoring depleted kelp beds, particularly near the large cities, Los Angeles and San Diego, where they have apparently incurred damage because of pollution. We've developed techniques for culturing kelp and transplanting it, protecting it from its enemies.

Kelp beds are the jungles of the sea, and productively they are very rich. Kelp creates a lot of food for animals. It provides shelter. A lot of things are attracted into these areas where the kelp plants grow. When the kelp bed disappears, some of these animals starve, others move away to find a habitat that's more suitable to them, and the ecological community just goes to pieces. What we've tried to do — and very successfully — is to restore some of the depleted kelp beds.

For a while, like 20 years ago, in certain areas the deterioration was alarming. There were 30 miles of kelp beds along the Palos Verdes coast that deteriorated completely. This was a big resource — a species of giant kelp — that was just completely eliminated, and people didn't know why. Some people thought it was just something that happened naturally. Other people blamed pollution from the big metropolitan areas. Other people claimed it was the harvesters that were killing it. Nobody really knew why. So the State put up some funds to get researchers out to find out why the kelp was disappearing.

We tried getting some of the sewage from the various outfalls and mixing that with sea water to give a ratio at which the kelp sees it out in the ocean — and the kelp just grew fine. It loved the nutrients that were in the sewage. What we found as the problem was that the sewage encouraged a grazing organism, the sea urchin.

The urchin looks like a pin cushion — it's got spines coming out all over — and it's a vegetarian. One of the favorite items in its diet is the kelp plant. You find urchins near the sewage outfalls just like locusts on a field of wheat. These armies of urchins would move along and just wipe out everything in their path — kelp and everything else. When the kelp was gone, the urchins would just sit around, and when the little plant would start to

Kelp bed near Gaviota, Santa Barbara County

grow back they'd pounce on it and eat it, so the kelp couldn't come back.

You could see this happening in the polluted areas, but you could also go out in a pure area, like in central California, or down in Baja California, and you'd see the urchins destroying underwater vegetation, so we couldn't really say that the polluted area was different from the clean area — until we watched them for several years. We found that in the clear areas the urchins would wipe out an acre of kelp forest, but then they'd starve to death, or march off and munch on kelp somewhere else, and the kelp would come back. But in the polluted areas the urchin population just persisted, and it turned out what they were living on was the organic matter from the sewage and this kept the population going.

The answer turned out to be to control the urchins. We got the diving clubs in Los Angeles organized, and got people with hammers going around and just bopping urchins, and it worked. We gradually whittled away on these populations, and the kelp came back. Lots of times we sped up the process by several years by bringing in large plants to produce spores so they could get little babies started in a hurry. The techniques proved so useful that the kelp harvesting companies now have five divers they hire full-time to go around and bop the urchins and keep the kelp beds in good shape.

We had a very important urchin predator all along the coast, 200 years ago — the sea otter. Sea otters ranged as far south as Baja California, gobbling up urchins. After the sea otters were killed by the fur trade, the urchins became out of balance. On the central California coast now, where the sea otter is making a comeback, you don't have any urchin problem.

What are some of the other animals that live along the coast underwater?

In a typical kelp bed you commonly have 300-400 species of animals: fish, lobsters, crab, abalone and scallops. Several species of interest to humans are becoming quite scarce. I remember when I was a boy in La Jolla; my family could invite ten people in for an abalone dinner or a lobster dinner, and a few hours before the guests would arrive you'd just get on your face mask and swim fins and pick them up. They were just everywhere. Nowadays it takes you two or three weeks to stock up your freezer with these things, and *then* you invite the guests. The abundance of lobster and abalone has decreased drastically, particularly in Southern California, because of the fishing pressure.

Then there's a whole range of fish which are just ornamental, like the Garibaldi, which is a bright orange color. It's often called the marine goldfish. They get to be about a foot long, and they're very colorful and beautiful, and they'll come up and bump your face mask if they think you're getting too close to their nest.

What are some of your favorite diving spots, the prettiest ones?

As a general rule, the prettiest diving areas are where you have a lot of vertical relief in the bottom topography, where you have pinnacles or submarine cliffs or canyons. That seems to attract marine life, and those areas tend to be the richest and most diverse. The La Jolla Submarine Canyon or the Carmel Submarine Canyon are two beautiful areas. Catalina Island and San Clemente Island have a lot of vertical relief underwater, mainly in the form of cliffs and caves. Some of the cliffs are 60 feet high, with caves that go back in them. Those are a lot of fun to prowl around.

You get further north, there's one very beautiful area, the Point Lobos State Reserve. The seaweeds that you get down here tend to be a little drab — they're mainly brown or yellow with a little bit of green — but you get up in central California and you get much more color in the seaweed. Some of them are irridescent blue and some are bright red, pink, in addition to the browns and the greens, and it makes a very colorful backdrop in which all these animals are swimming around.

Another pretty area is Mission Beach, just about a mile north of Point Lobos, where the Monterey Submarine Canyon comes closest to the shore. It comes within 200 feet of the beach. You can put on your scuba gear and swim right out and look over the edge of the canyon, and it's really beautiful, it's spectacular. You have to take things a little bit at a time — you can only see 30 or 40 feet — but once you get into that framework, you see a canyon wall with soft corals coming out of it and starfish draped over it and brightly colored anemones. Some of the anemones and corals have a fluorescence — they take in light of one wavelength, say blue light, and then emit light of another wavelength, say yellow or orange. They look like little flames because they're giving out this orange or red light, sitting down there in a very drab environment.

Another feature of the underwater is the amount of motion that goes on. It's as if the wind were always blowing. But with the wind it blows in one direction. The motion underwater is primarily wave surge, which goes in one direction as the wave crest passes over and then it goes back in the other direction as the trough passes over you. So there's a back and forth sweeping. It's very graceful to see the longer seaweeds swaying back and forth. Everything is very dynamic.

Are you optimistic or pessimistic about the future of the underwater coastal eco-system?

I think I'm optimistic. I don't think we'll ever return to the completely pristine character that existed 300 or 400 years ago, because we'll always have a lot of fishing going on, and some waste disposal, however discreetly it's handled. But I think we've seen the low point, which probably occurred around 1960. We now have much more understanding of how the marine environment works, and all the time we're getting more and more scientific information, and understanding more of what we're doing to it — and modifying our actions. I've seen a definite improvement in the last 15 years. □

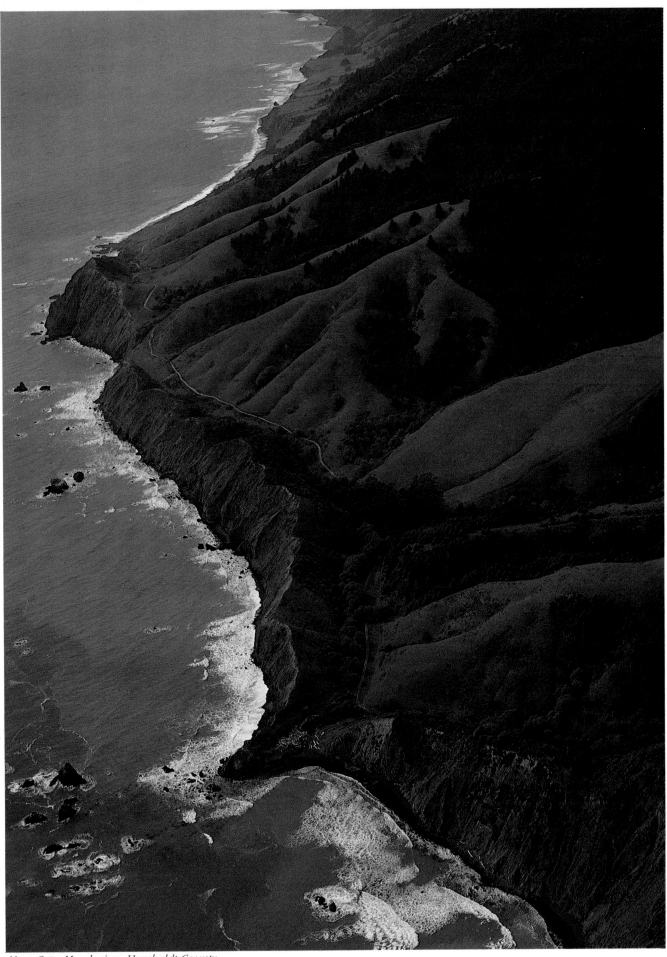

Near Cape Mendocino, Humboldt County

Crystal Cove and the San Joaquin Hills, the last piece of undeveloped coastline in Orange County

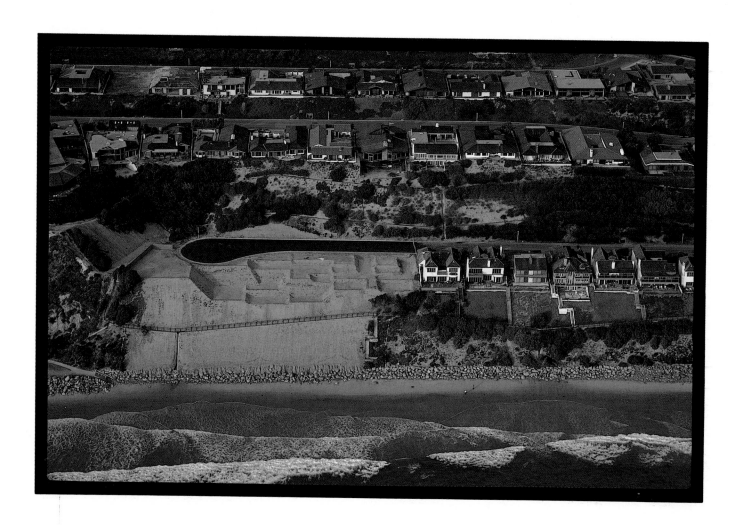

Dana Point, Orange County

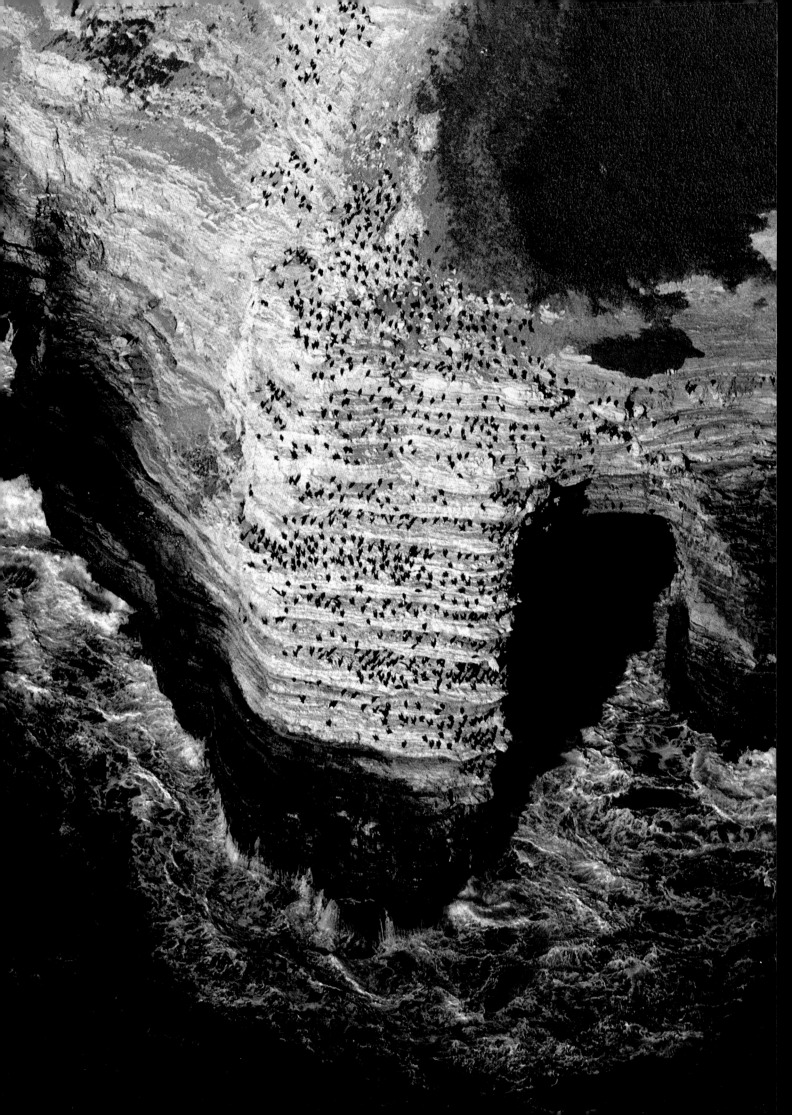

Left: Near Point Arguello, Vandenberg Air Force Base

Deserted offshore well near Coal Oil Point, Santa Barbara County

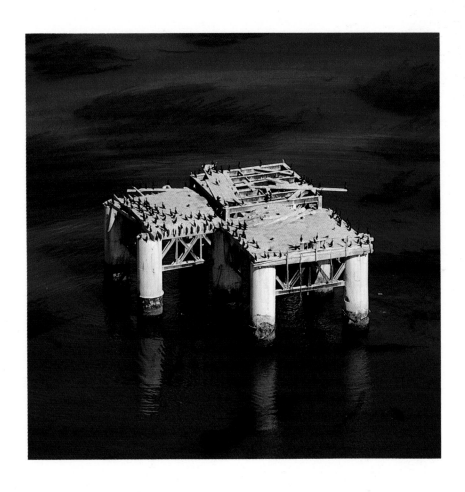

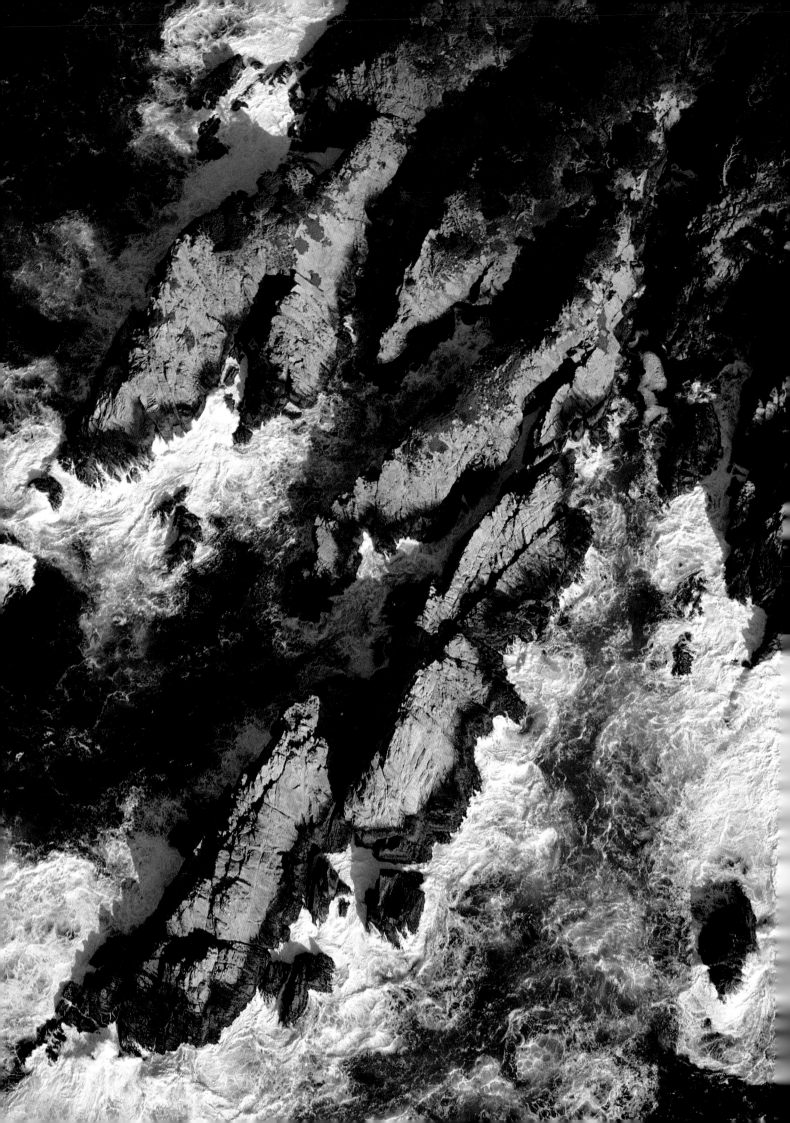

Ansel Adams

Generations have learned what California looks like through his eyes. But Ansel Adams is more than simply a photographer. He is a fighter. Early in the going, his reverence for his subject — the natural beauty and drama of the West — impelled Adams toward the Sierra Club and the environmental movement. His enthusiasm drew him from battle to battle, and this momentum continues today. Adams campaigns at every opportunity on behalf of legislation which would protect his home turf, Big Sur, from indiscriminate development. Despite his white beard, Adam's excitement about his craft and art seems that of a much younger person. A sense that many more discoveries lie ahead for him pervades. He is quick to point out that he is best known for his mountain and high country photography. Yet many of his coast images are masterworks, especially those taken at Point Lobos. Any tour of his favorite photo sites on the California coast starts with Point Lobos.

P oint Lobos is a gem. It's a reserve, and the name "reserve" is very important. "Park" means recreation and hot dog stands, pretty girlies, masses of people. Point Lobos is really *reserved* for its intrinsic qualities. There's nothing there but picnic benches.

The Point Lobos ranger tells a funny story about keeping photographers from wandering off the trails by explaining to them that Ansel Adams never strays from the marked paths.

It's true. Edward Weston photographed all over the place when he first came. Then as visitation picked up, the damage to the terrain was pretty obvious. Weston had to agree that cabling off the trails was necessary. Otherwise the visitors would just run down the hillside slopes. So he agreed to give up his total freedom, and I've always thought it was right. They have been a little restrictive, but it is for the good of the place. I know there are some beautiful trees a hundred feet down below Cypress Point, but you can't have everything.

There are other good photographic sites along the coast. Beginning up north at the Oregon border there are spectacular rock and shore images — just over the border. The first reserve, Patrick's Point, is quite a remarkable place. There's a great expanse of beach, miles and miles long with wonderful storm conditions; every time I've seen it the breakers are half a mile wide. It's terrific. From Crescent City down, there are exciting beaches. South of Eureka, there's rugged land with many fine beaches and beautiful configurations and driftwood sights. An incredible collection of rocks around Elk. It's fairly spectacular at Bodega Head. The town of Bodega is quaint. There's a University of California marine biology plant at Bodega Head — wonderful little set-up, beautiful little building, important study.

From Bodega south it's very spectacular, with Tomales Bay — the whole Point Reyes peninsula is wonderful, wild all the way to Olema. Then Bolinas and then the Marin Headlands — simply marvelous. Then there's the San Francisco side, from Lands End; that view north across the Golden Gate is probably one of the most beautiful in the world. All you see is rolling hills and maybe a little lighthouse.

All Route One down to Santa Cruz has some beautiful places — there are tons of rock that go out and out at Nuevo Point. There's a power plant near Moss Landing, and it's quite beautiful in there, but Monterey Bay isn't much until you get to Point Lobos. Then there's the Big Sur coast all the way down to San Simeon. Pismo Beach, further down, is horrible. Then Nipomo Dunes and on to Point Sal. Beyond Point Sal there's not much of quality that hasn't been built up — into Los Angeles and Palos Verdes Estates. There might be a few points of photographic interest on that part of the coast, but I can't remember any.

I've been all around these places, but I don't necessarily have important good pictures of everywhere. You just have to expose yourself. Something I've seen that might be especially beautiful for me — you might get there at a bad time, or you might get there at a time when you'd see a wonderful aspect of the place that I've missed.

You have difficulty with the summer fog which is almost universal on the entire coast. From the air you might find interesting fog patterns. From the air, the water has a low luminous quality, and the white is very white, so with ordinary color film you get high contrast, unfortunately high contrast. Early and late in the day, and in winter, when you have low sun, working into the sun can be most revealing. At Point Lobos, from the air all you see is a jagged hand — the promontory — sticking out, with blaring white water and extremely dark blue water with white surf. Extremely blue-black water.

William E. Colby created the California Parks system. He did a wonderful job. I remember going all around with him back in the '20s and '30s. We've had several conservation battles in this state. Redwood country. North rivers. One of the biggest scraps for the Sierra Club was over the Marin Headlands. The developers were very

Point Lobos State Reserve, near Carmel

strong in wanting that Marin Headlands area there at the Golden Gate for a big apartment complex, to be called Marincello. I was instrumental in that battle. I made a big enlargement of the view up the coast, with beautiful clouds, and an architect friend made really exact scale drawings of the proposed Marincello buildings and pasted them onto the photograph, just where they'd be. That was shown around the Bay Area, and it helped no end when people really saw — "My god, is *that* how this would look?" Marincello was never built.

The next big battle was with the Atlantic-Richfield oil company, over the building of a Moss landing refinery. The developers told the Monterey people that putting industry there would give an enormous advantage, tax-wise and labor-wise. We kept saying that the effluvia and the fumes from a big industrial development would play havoc with the last clean valley in the state. It was proved to the farmers that if an industrial complex went in there, burning coal and producing chemical fumes far in excess of what comes from an honest refinery, damage to the crops would be great. We convinced the oil company and the developers that their image was at stake, and they got out. Pacific Gas & Electric is there now with a power plant, and they do a pretty good job; it's quite clean. They burn heavy oil at night when the wind is out to sea, and they burn refined, low-sulfur oil in the daytime; so the pollution is not considerable.

You don't see the dangerous pollutants in the air; what you see very often is the steam emissions. The colder the weather the more steam. Steam is like tracer bullets — it tells you where the *real* pollution is going.

The next big fight was the Big Sur. That was a major one, and we lost it. Temporarily. The Cranston Bill — if it had gotten to the Senate — would have put the area under the Forest Service's control. The Service would have had first choice on land purchases; as long as a rancher wanted to ranch and run his cattle it was fine, but if he wanted to sell it for condominiums, the Forest Service could have moved in. That had the opposition of Senator Hayakawa *and* the redneck opposition, and the marijuana growers opposition. The marijuana growers didn't want any Feds around whatsoever. But Cranston says his Big Sur bill is coming back, and these people are going to find they can't control the coast themselves; it can be protected.

The developers want to take over. We point out how South Lake Tahoe looks — I had tried to do something about South Lake Tahoe in the Sierra Club. In just a few fast years, South Tahoe had a complete and total urbanization — highrises, casinos — the lake is suffering. There's been movement after movement to protect the lake, and it's always killed by developers.

You once wrote that the process of urbanization that has destroyed and blighted so much natural beauty isn't evil so much as a sickness of modern man.

It's a complete lack of appreciation of the land. A violent selfishness of the moment. No thought of the future at all. The machinery of development today is overpowering. Once a lot of money comes into a place, the earth moves, and an enormous damage can be done that is not reparable.

I've seen pictures from the air of smog in the San Francisco Bay that are terrifying. With certain winds, it'll blow right down to Monterey through Santa Clara and we'll have smog. It's come out here. One morning after several days of north winds I went out to get the sunrise, and I saw shafts of sunlight coming down through the hills through the smog, all hazy. It was a frightening experience.

The tragedy is that increasing smog controls are offset by increasing population. Now this government wants to take off some smog controls! They don't give a damn; just make a buck. As long as we have fossil fuels burning we're going to have smog; as long as we have gasoline cars that aren't highly controlled we're going to have smog.

There's a terrific number of extreme right-wingers in this area. I'm in a nest of inconsolables. They're a type of American who says, "Goddammit, I'm an American citizen. *I'm* not going to build anything on my lot on the coast. *I* don't want to spoil anything, but, goddammit, I want the *right* to do it." On the other hand, the Coastal Commission did grievous harm to its reputation, because they prevented people from using their property — and without compensation, and that's very bad. If you had a lot up here for 25 years that you wanted to build on when you retired and found you couldn't, you should receive some recompense. The Commission hadn't any money, the federal government couldn't do it, so the opponents said, "When the Feds come in, they'll just take your land and won't pay you a cent." They would just love to get rid of the Coastal Commission and just come in and build whatever they please, because they claim if you own the land, you have the right to do whatever you want with it. □

Near Fan Shell Beach on the Seventeen Mile Drive, Monterey

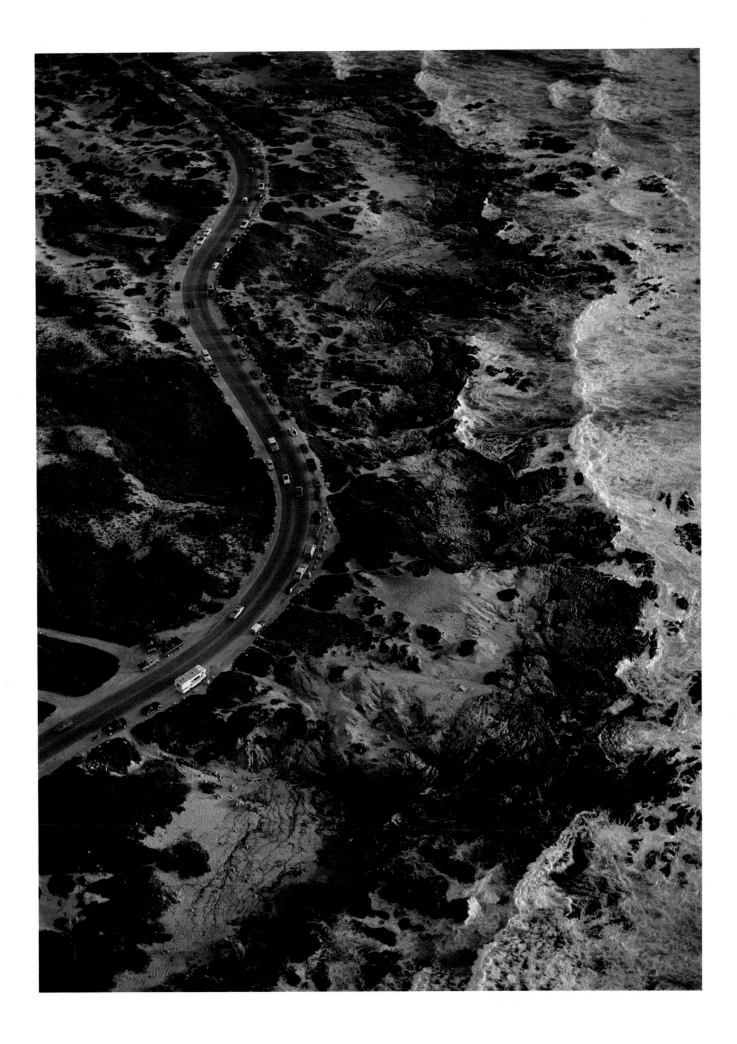

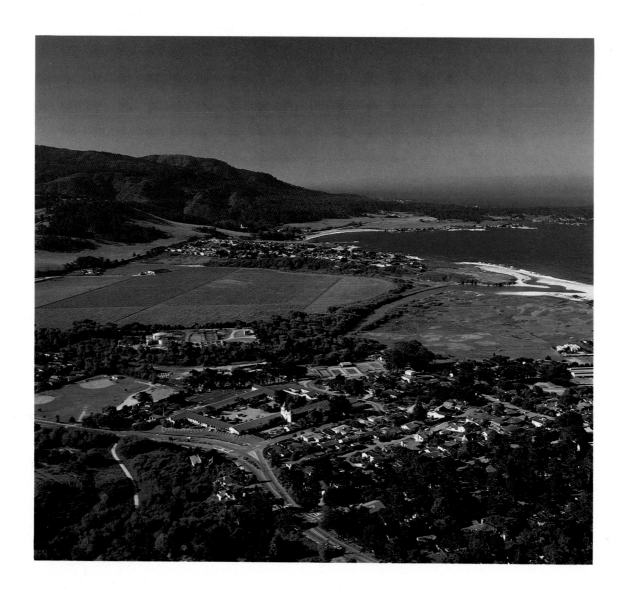

Odello Artichoke Patch, Carmel River State Park

Right: Looking northwest from 3,000 feet above northern Santa Cruz County

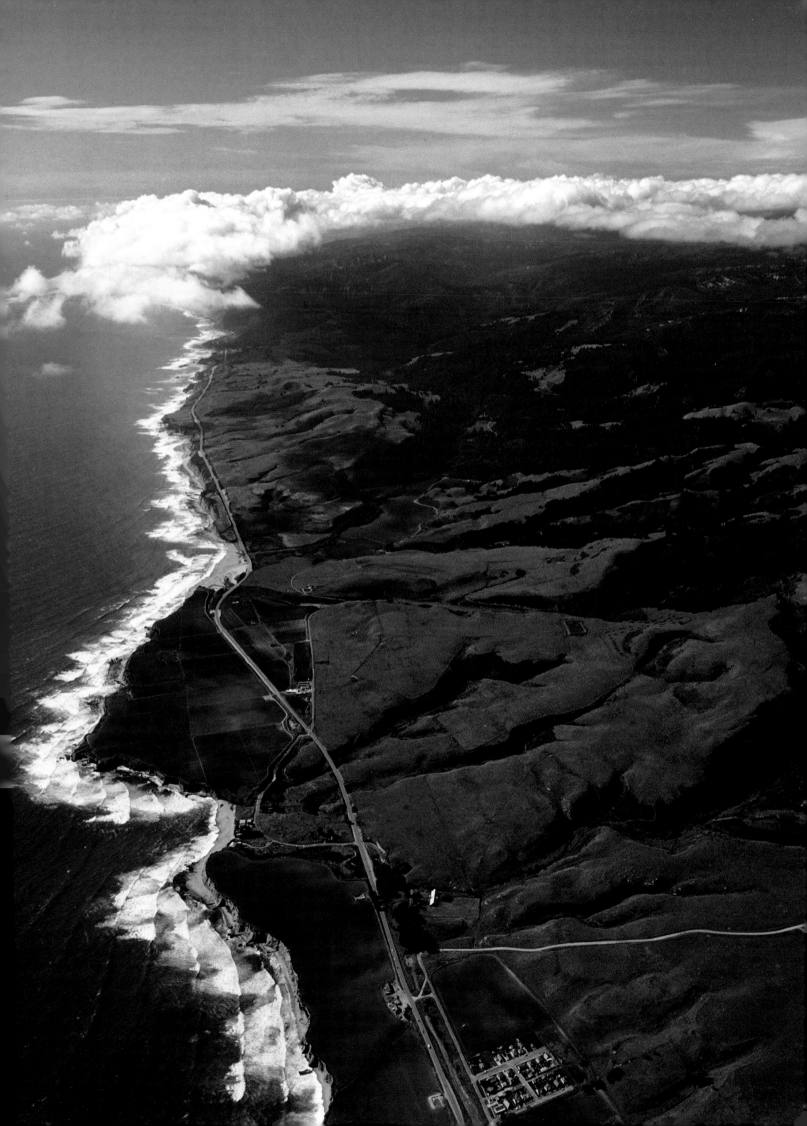

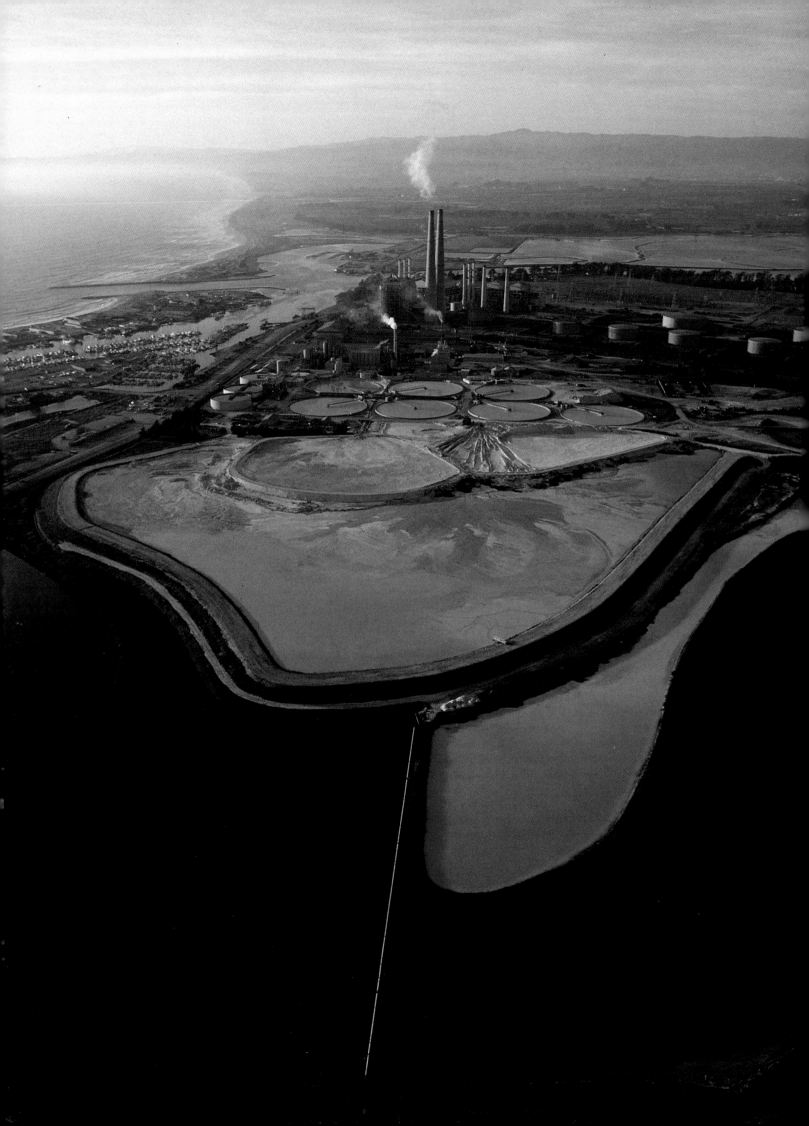

Left: Magnesia and brick plants, and electric generating facility, Moss Landing on Monterey Bay

Loading container cargo, Southeast Basin, Port of Long Beach

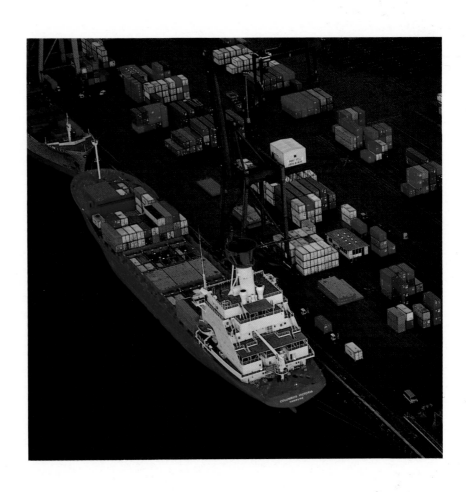

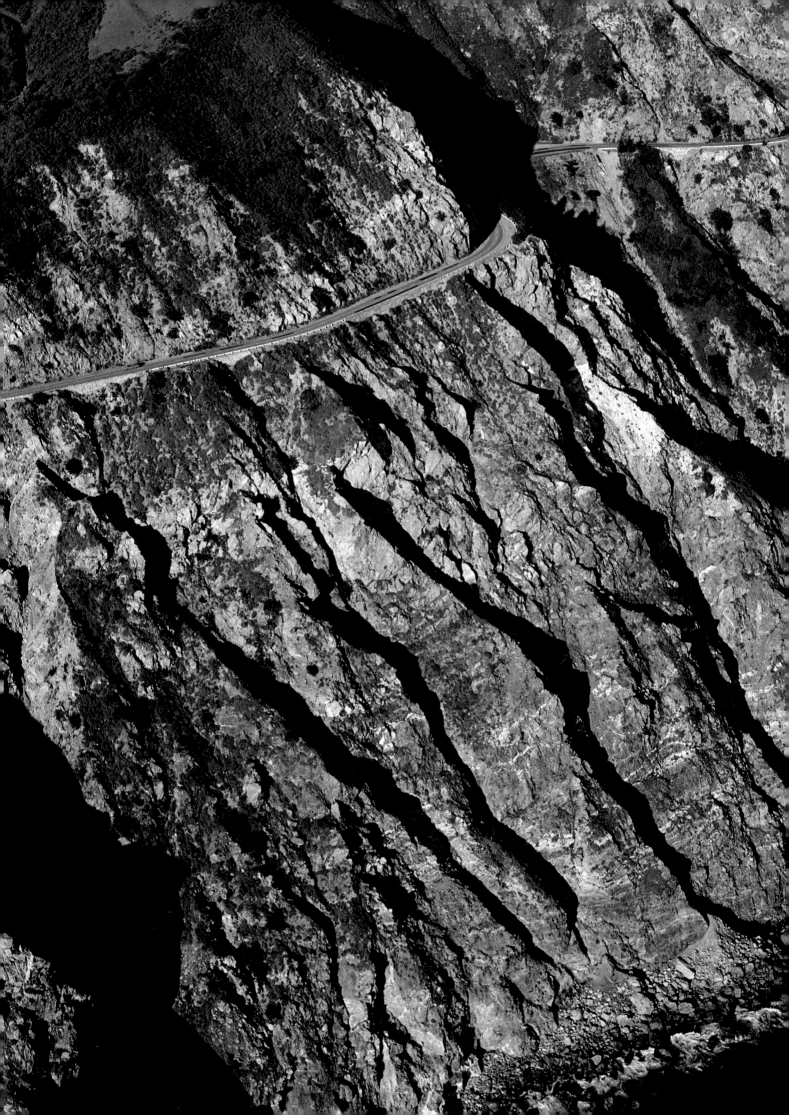

CONSTRUCTION OF HIGHWAY 1

Tom Neff

*In 1919, the California Assembly approved plans
to build California Highway One through
some of the most beautiful, and rugged terrain
in the world — the central coast region known as
Big Sur. It took nine years, however, before
appropriations and engineering plans were
completed and construction could begin. That
highway was part of Tom Neff's life even before
there was a roadbed. Neff started working on
the road's survey crew in 1924 "as a flagman,
transitman and, later, chief of the survey party."
When construction began in 1928, Neff went to
the construction camps as a "freeman" among the
mostly convict labor force. Neff retired a few
years ago having spent his last 18 years with the
highway department as maintenance super-
intendent of the 40 or 50 miles of road he and
others spent 13 years building.*

The first camp we had was up on the Little Sur
River and then we moved down to Ander-
son Canyon camp. I guess I was there about
three years. There were about 150 men
in the camp. There were cabins for the 25 or so "freemen"
and the convicts lived in tents.

The freemen were the shovel operators and truck
drivers and on the engineering crew. The convicts did the
day labor. I think they got about $2 a day, but deductions
were taken out for their meals and lodging. I guess
they ended up with about 75 cents a day for their work.
Some of those fellows ended up with a nice piece of
change when they got out, good for those days anyway,
maybe around a thousand dollars.

Normally, we'd get on the job at 8:00 or so in the
morning, work for eight hours and then hike back to camp,
which might be three or four miles. Sometimes it wasn't
far in a straight line, but it had a lot of ups and
downs. California One is sometimes 50 feet from the surf
line, and it can climb to 1,000 feet above sea level.
Once in a while, when the days were shorter, we'd knock
off a little early, but I only remember one time when
we stopped work. That was when the wind was blowing so
hard we couldn't get anything done.

We had three power shovels and trucks. Mostly it was
just blastin' and diggin' and casting the dirt over the
side. Of course it was a lot of rock up there. Lots of
shooting — dynamiting — went on.

A couple of convicts got killed on the job. When the
dirt was dumped over the edge it made a pile that
looked like you could walk down it, but the dirt wasn't
compacted, so you couldn't stand on it; you'd slip right
down. A couple of guys tried to walk down the pile
and away they went.

Did the camps get wild? No. No, everyone was so tired
you could look out after 9:00 at night and there wouldn't
be a light in the camp. It was awfully hard work.

On Sundays we would do our laundry in the morning
and in the afternoon we would hike the hills. I was
young and wound pretty tight in those days. We'd hike
the hills looking for homesteaders' cabins. Hearst had
bought up all that land and people just abandoned
their cabins and packed their stuff out on horses. We
cruised the hills looking for cabins and old magazines
in 'em.

When the road was finished — and it was only graded,
no paving — there were two celebrations, one at each
end. Up north they put a big boulder out in the road
and drilled a hole in it. A powder monkey loaded it and
they set off a shot and shattered the boulder. That
was quite an event for us. □

State Highway #1 near Big Sur

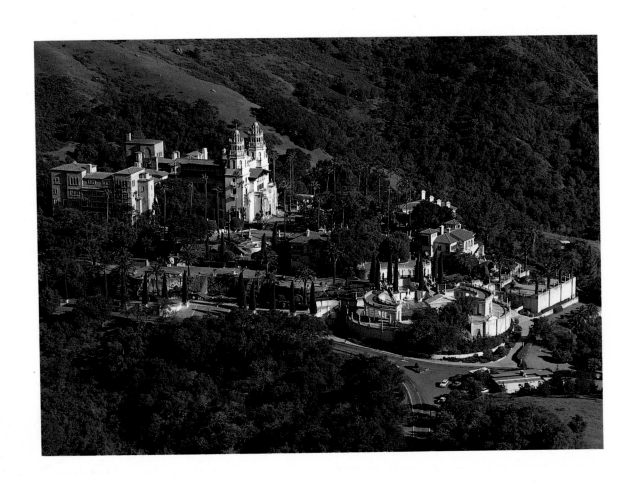

Hearst Castle, San Simeon State Historical Monument

Right: Hearst Castle is dwarfed by the Santa Lucia mountains

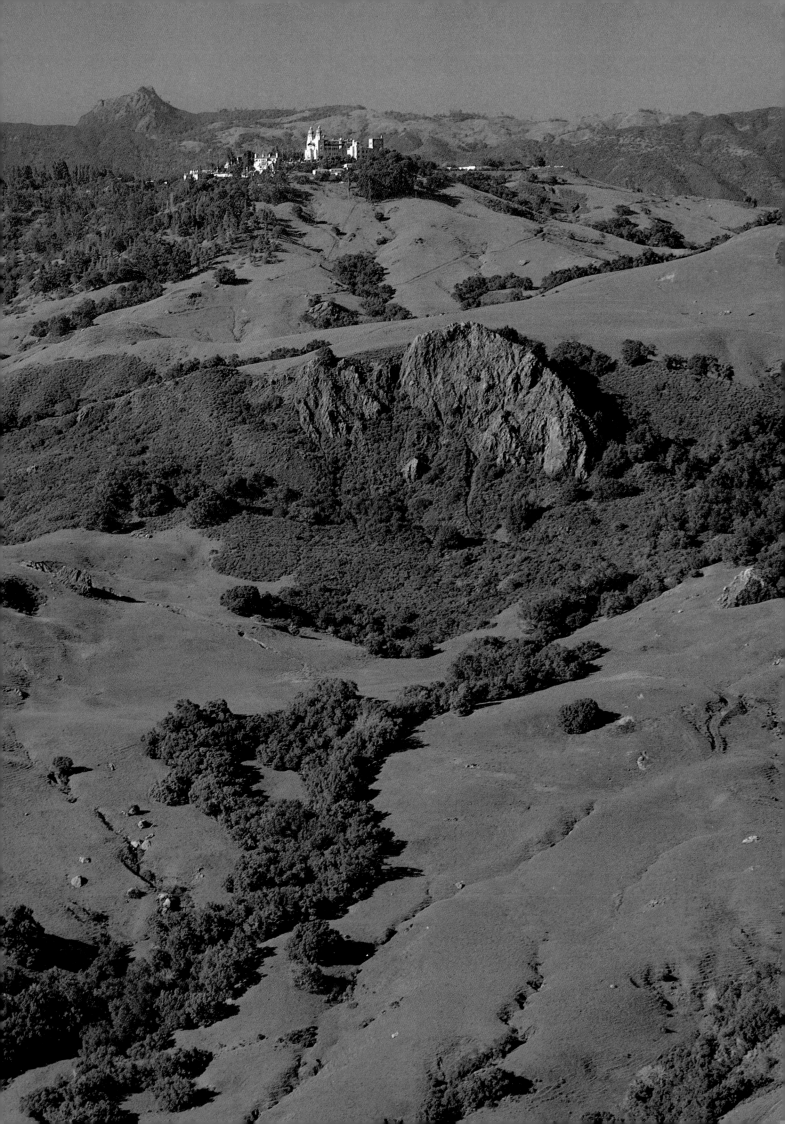

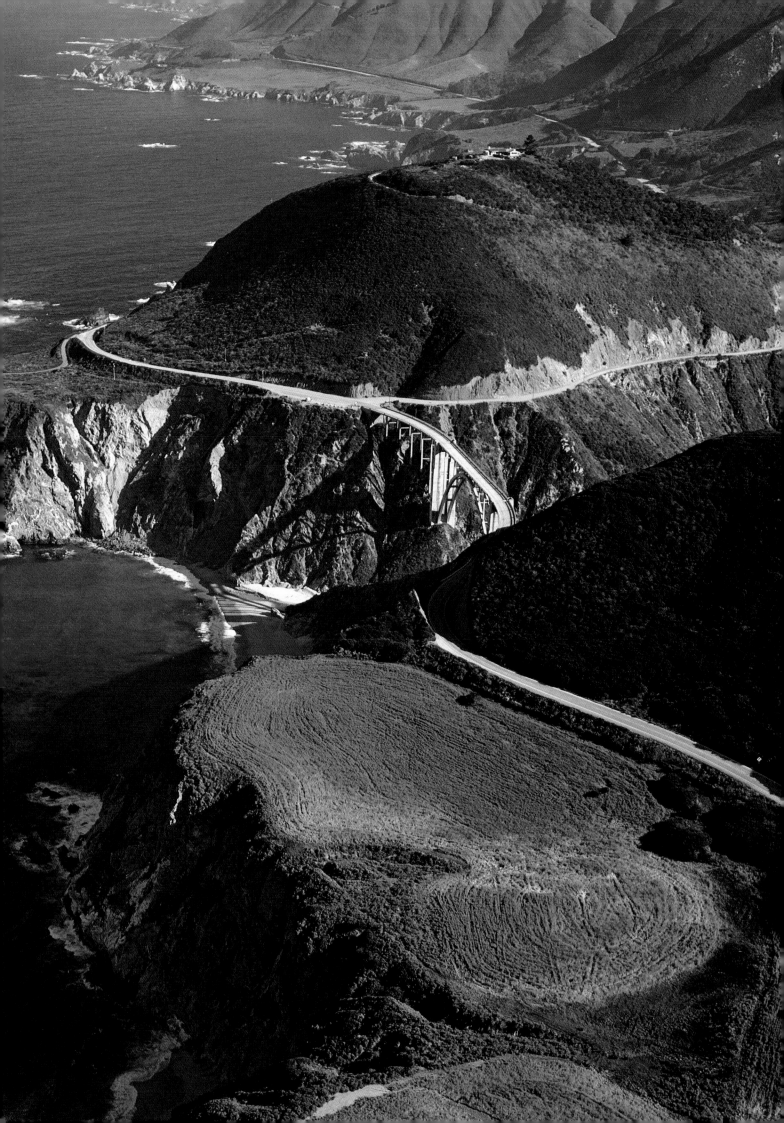

HIGHWAY PATROLMAN

Ken Wright

One of the most rugged stretches of the Coast Highway passes through Big Sur, on north to Little Sur. Because of the remoteness of this area from the California Highway Patrol's regional office in Salinas, it was made a "resident post" in 1959, meaning that the patrolman lived near Highway One year-round. Due to an increase in tourist traffic, the CHP upgraded it to a two-man post in 1970. Ken Wright has been with the CHP for 13 years, the last 10 as resident traffic officer living in Big Sur. He loves it there — both the coast and the highway itself.

It's a fun road to drive because it's beautiful. I've never tired of driving the road. There's always something new to see in the different seasons. You're seeing it in a different way. Early mornings in the fall and spring it's great to go down the coast at 6:30 or so in the morning and the sun's just coming up and you're looking at the shadows and hues and colors, and, in the summertime, some of the gorgeous sunsets. You never get tired of looking at it. Even the big storms, the waves. . . .

You know, everybody can *talk* about the waves crashing and you can read Robinson Jeffers, you can read Eric Barker, and you can read all the great poets that wrote about the coast, but you really have got to *see* it. I've not read much of Jeffers or Barker, et cetera, but you can understand what they're trying to write about because they've seen something that's really fantastic.

When it becomes wintertime, that's the savage, primitive time. When wintertime comes, that's when you find out who's gonna stay and who isn't. You take a tough winter here where we get 40 or 50 inches of rain, or the electrical power goes out for four or five days, like it was two years ago just before Christmas; they go through these inconveniences and you find out who's gonna stay and who's gonna leave. A lot of people leave. You get these tourist-oriented transient workers and they're here for a year, maybe two, and they move on because they get tired of the ups and downs of the coast.

Have you had any run-ins with people down here where you suddenly found yourself in danger?

I went through a shooting incident nine years ago. It wasn't a traffic stop. I wound up being shot and shooting an individual and he was taken into custody.

It happened up on what we call the old county road, which was the original road into Big Sur. That's a dirt road, still there and still passable. Nice drive, pretty drive, you get a different perspective of the coast. The sheriff's office was down the road on a cattle rustling call or something and we had a call about a guy shooting people. The call is not unusual; I mean, down here in '72 with the tail end of the hippie era, it was a common thing. People living in the area oftentimes shot at people they didn't like.

Anyway, this guy was three and a half miles up the old county road and he was parked in a car. It's a twisty, windy road with a lot of redwood trees along the edge of the road, and I was coming up a small hill that makes a curve. He was parked behind the redwood trees. As I approached him in the car I was thinking that this could possibly be the guy, this is possibly the individual. I'm slowly closing on this guy and suddenly the war is on, just about that quick.

He started shooting with a 30-30 out the window. He had his driver's window rolled down. He hit the car, and I got hit, pieces of bullet in the chin, the side of my jaw and a piece in the eye. It happened very quickly. I probably said "Oh shit!" a lot for two or three seconds. I pulled my revolver out and started shooting back. I've got the car door open but I stay in the car because the car offers protection. Took my revolver out and fired several rounds which went absolutely nowhere because I wasn't paying attention. After a while, the mechanism takes over that you've been working with for a long time: you're gonna have to shoot this guy, you're gonna have to get on this situation. This all happens within a couple of seconds. You're not thinking. But all of a sudden I said to myself, "You better start paying attention." And that's when I shot the guy. And went on to get him arrested and the deputy showed up. I was off work for six weeks.

Are there any parts of the highway that seem to be particularly dangerous?

Well, in terms of losing your life by going over the side, yes, there are: the cliffs. The road runs from sea level to 1,200 or 1,400 feet above the ocean. There are some areas where if you go off in an automobile there's a good possibility that you're not going to live. There are always exceptions to the rule. There's a young man I know down the coast who drove a car 700 or 800 feet to the ocean and got out and walked away from it with nothing more than some damage to his hand. Of course, you like to point to those stories, but then there's the other occasion when a guy goes down 300 feet and is dead.

Our fatal picture goes up and down. One year, in 1976, we had 14 fatals on the coast and the next year we had

Bixby Creek Bridge in the early morning, with state Highway #1 to the left and the unpaved old Coast Road to the right

eight and the year before that we had maybe six or seven. But this highway insists upon your paying attention to it. It's not a highway that you can drive and be very lax about. The element that you have to be watching for is the tourists. You can come around a blind curve and there will be a guy standing in the middle of the road taking a picture of what he feels to be a beautiful sight. And it *is* a beautiful sight. But he or she is so enraptured with what they're looking at that they forget they're on a highway where other people are driving.

You see tourists from all over the world. Is it true that New Yorkers are the worst drivers?

My partner and I both feel this. Invariably we'll come up with a story about: "You should have seen the turkey I stopped the other day" — which is perhaps not the correct way to describe somebody, but policemen say things like that. And then you proceed to tell the story about what the turkey did and we will always look at one another and say, "Well, he's from New York, right?" And yep, almost invariably. New York drivers, as opposed to West Coast drivers, probably don't drive much, so they don't have the exposure of being on a road and driving the different experiences. Some of them are aggressive, which over the years I've learned comes from being in New York. It's inherited, I guess. From their environment. New Yorkers just tend to be lousy drivers.

On the other hand, California drivers don't signal enough. California drivers get tickets for not signalling. You would be surprised how many automobile accidents we investigate on this coast where the contributing factor in a passing situation is the lack of signalling. They're just assuming that somebody else is looking out for them, and it's not necessarily going to happen.

We have a print-out that says the road from Little Sur to Hurricane Point has more fatals on it. It's an up-grade road with a lot of curves in it and Hurricane is a popular viewing point, and also one of the higher terrain areas on the coast. It's 1,000 feet to the ocean right at Hurricane. As you come down from Hurricane going south towards Little Sur it drops and we have people driving off there.

And I don't know if this is something you want to report or not, but a lot of those accidents are suicides. Some are real suicides and some aren't. The difference is a witness driving behind somebody and watching him accelerate as he gets to a certain point and goes over and off. The difference is finding out that a guy has incurable cancer and has been missing for six or eight months and then the body turns up here. The difference is a daylight accident — smooth tracks, no braking accident, no evasive action whatsoever — and someone goes off.

The thing that bothers me, or that I wonder about, is why do they come down here to do it? You're talking about a gorgeous place, a place that people really like, and why add that stigma to the coast? Why take a gorgeous place and put a self-destruct mechanism into it? □

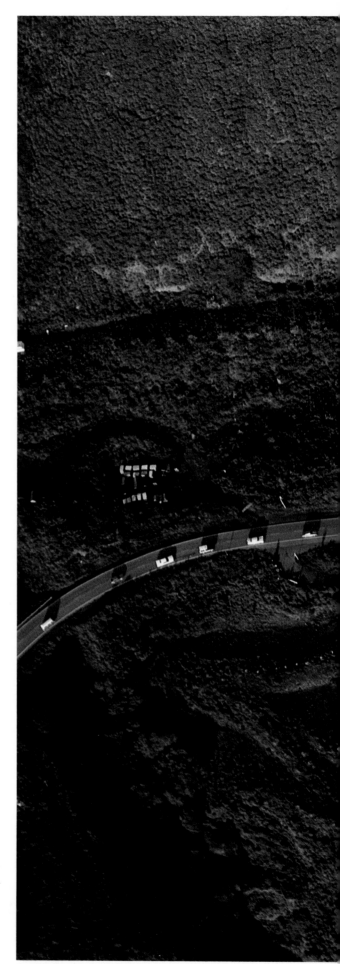

Traffic along state Highway #1, Monterey County

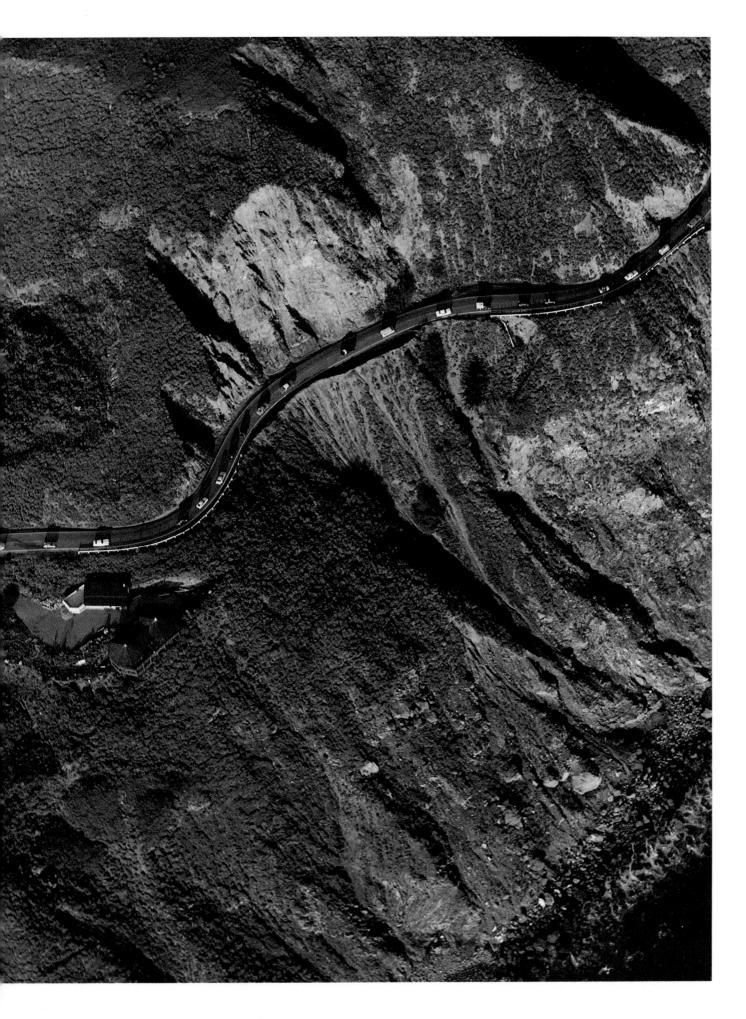

Lolly and Bill Fassett

*Lolly Fassett's father helped found the coastal
hamlet of Carmel on Monterey Bay, in its earliest
days an artists' colony. Bill Fassett started
Carmel's first newspaper, called* What's Doing
In Carmel. *By the time they purchased the plot of
land where later would stand Nepenthe — a
sort of living room for the Big Sur region's creative
spirits — they had five kids to feed and were
not long on cash. Back then, coastal acreage
didn't require much cash. More recently, in an
old log cabin on the Nepenthe property, thick
with vases and glasses of all sorts and weird
feathers and wonderful beatnik junk, Lolly
recalled Nepenthe's origins with nostalgia.
Bill, meanwhile, was glued to a baseball game
on a black and white television set. He spoke out
of the corner of his mouth, chain smoking, his
eyes rarely leaving the screen. He and Lolly,
he said, had lived in San Francisco, liked it, but
missed the rugged splendor of the Big Sur
coast. So not long after World War II they began
looking for property in earnest.*

Bill: We soon discovered this old log house, then called
the Trails Club. It was built by a group of Christian
Science-Sierra Club type people who used to go down
before and during World War I and rent horses and
ride down the coast, when you could have bought anything for about 15 bucks an acre. And then a lot of them
built their own houses down there. In 1944, Orson
Welles and Rita Hayworth had done a bond selling
trip and war bond deal in San Francisco. He was with
his old friend from the Mercury Theater, Joseph Cotten,
and their agent; I think there were six of them, the
men and their wives. They were just sort of meandering
along the coast and they saw the side road and they
drove up and saw this log cabin and fell in love with it,
and made some inquiries around and found out they
could buy it. The people that had built it had gone off
and built their own homes on some land just above it.
Welles wanted to come up and write, and it was only
a few hours from Hollywood. By '45, you know, they'd
gotten a divorce and the property passed to Rita,
and she was romancing with the Ali Khan and didn't need
no country property. So we made our own inquiries and
found out that it could be bought and we bought it
in 1947. We didn't know what we'd do but I figured
I'd do something, build some cabins or something.
There were no restrictions then like there is now. It took
quite a while before we finally got ownership of it and

then I went to find any kind of work I could do: building
bridges, working on the highway. The standard wage
was about $1.50 an hour; it was tough feeding the kids but
life was cheap because you didn't go out anywhere.
You'd buy a pair of blue jeans every year. Had interesting
neighbors like Henry Miller. Sometimes he'd leave his
kids there. We thought we'd be isolated but so many
people we hardly knew, or friends of friends, dropped in
on us. When we started, there weren't many motels
and we were like running a restaurant, so I said to my
wife, "That's what we ought to do, we ought to start
a restaurant." There was no fun place to go in Big Sur
where you could have a drink and there was a lot of
distinguished people there.

Lolly: Henry Miller used to come down and play ping
pong a lot. And he could never beat Bill and it would
just drive him crazy. He sent Bill a book on Zen. *The Zen
of Archery* or something. He came down one night at
10:00 o'clock and he said, "I want to play ping pong with
you, I figured it out, I'm gonna beat you." Bill beat him.
He wouldn't change his serve. Miller was a remarkable
ping pong player but he would never change his serve.
Whereas these guys, when they were playing in com-
petition, their serves were outrageous. That extraordinary
group of people, playing ping pong! I was amazed
because they were all intellectuals, artists and just
absolutely loved that game. They'd play it until 3:00
o'clock in the morning, just never stop.

Bill: I was my own bartender. One day I looked up and
there was a fabulous collection: Anais Nin, Man Ray and
Miller. Another time Brendan Behan came. He said that
when his play first opened on Broadway he heard it
was good swimming over in the East River, so he went
over there and he said he took off his clothes and then all
these little Eastside kids knew he wasn't Jewish. Another
time I was sitting at the bar, just me and two people.
Dylan Thomas and his wife Caitlan. Dylan kept doodling
— I should have kept those things. Made little drawings.
I never had a discussion with him. He just stared at me
drunk as hell. He'd been to a literary tea and he said,
"Where could I go?" They said, "Go down to Nepenthe,
that's the nearest bar to Paris." And Caitlan and I had a
great talk. She suffered a lot, you could see. He looked . . .
in three months I heard he was dead. He looked like hell.
You could see that he was suffering too. It must not be
easy for a rather attractive young woman to be married
to a genius.

How did you get the idea to build this restaurant?

Bill: Like I say, so many people dropped in on us, we
were trying to think what to do. And we could see that

Evening fog along the Santa Lucia mountains near Partington Point, Monterey County there would be more distinguished people coming. It's a fantastic place for older people to retire who have always been used to living in wild beautiful places or having second homes. And also we knew there would be a great tourist trade there; it's a marvelous location, probably one of the greatest places in the world to have a restaurant.

Lolly: We probably have one of the most dramatic settings anybody can have. We have a 40 mile view. On moonlit nights it's unbelievable, when the fog comes in and you see all those jagged trees out of the fog. There's constant magic here and constant change. The Phoenix roof — have you ever gone down and sat there? We've had weddings down there. What a place to get married! It's like another world.

Bill: We were a little ahead of our time. We had a reading of modern poetry the opening day. Had a buffet, forgot to collect from half the people. Five hundred people showed up. The next day I got a lot of waiters and bartenders and nobody showed up. That's the way it went for the first four years. We didn't cut it at all, and I had to go out and get a job and make money somewhere. But then eventually when they opened the Hearst Castle, that put us on the map and now we're just swarmed under.

Who was the architect?

Bill: We had a friend, Rowan Maiden, who had spent a lot of time at Taliesin with Frank Lloyd Wright, who was really a very talented guy. It won some sort of an architectural prize in a European magazine as a classic example of a small business in America. Among our first clients were architects from everywhere. They'd heard about it. It's typical Wright structure. As you can tell, when you see it, it has Frank Lloyd Wright written all over it. But it's uniquely Rowan Maiden's work.

Lolly: Rowan Maiden started designing and figuring that this was the best spot for the light and the sun and the whole thing, so we excavated. Dug out the hill and made the shelf that Nepenthe and the terrace are on. And then we had quite a time getting the plans through; people were really dubious about our plans but somebody said, "Oh well, Bill Fassett, just leave him alone . . ."

Was it hard to build it?

Bill: Very difficult, yeah. Because he did intricate trusses. You know, there were no schools of architecture when Wright was studying. But there were engineering schools and that made him, because he was then free to follow his own way. But he had a sound engineering background and that really liberated him, not going to a school of architecture. But being a good engineer, he understood stress. And all his stuff — he said everything should be functional. There's not a board in there that isn't

essential, but it's the way they do it, the Wright people.

It took about a year and a half to build. We started in the winter, '47-'48, and we opened in the spring of '49. There was a continued growing amount of tourists. When we went down there, cars were rationed and it was not easy, nobody ever heard of Big Sur to speak of. Now it's world famous. We've always appealed to sort of the intellectual, the relatively affluent nuclear physicists, teachers, professors. I mean now it has broad appeal; people just go there like going to the Grand Canyon. In those days people went out of their way that were literary and creative. Painters, artists, sculptors, ballet dancers.

What does the coast mean to Nepenthe?

Bill: Well, it's what it meant to us, really. I might contrast to the guy that came along years later that built a place called Ventana across the road. Makes an awful lot of money. He did essentially what we did for about fifty times as much money. He took a whole concept of a sophisticated city restaurant and inn and just set 'em down. I told him, look, start slow and let it grow organically like Nepenthe. We didn't build the shop till years later. And we agreed with the architect that it should — it was all local wood, we made the adobe bricks ourselves, and it fit the mountains and the sea and someone called it the greatest meeting of sea and land in the world. We felt that it should fit the country, which is so extraordinary. It shouldn't intrude. It should be part of it, made of local redwood, local pine, local certain types of decomposed granite that we made the adobe brick.

We'd never been in the restaurant business. It was like that Frank Lloyd Wright thing I was talking about. We had no previous experience, although I'd gone to the Hotel School at Cornell, in '31, '32.

Lolly: Our daughter Holly is running Nepenthe now. She's doing quite a job. She grew up through the ranks. What's happened now is that the people who used to work here, many of them have had children and those children are working here. We always seem to have youngsters wanting to work here and looking forward to it. That's what keeps the feeling here. All our little kids run around with pads and they're learning how to write up what people want and when they play, they play restaurant. Pretty soon they're in the restaurant. Now we have a new rash of new babies — an incredible amount of new babies. In the office we have a bassinet and sometimes in the kitchen we have a bassinet. So it's a huge overgrown family.

Bill: I've never had a passion for anything besides the restaurant. I'm still trying to write a book about it all, and I find it very difficult. I think what is needed is what Faulkner called a demon on his back, because everybody's lazy, you know. I'm always fascinated when somebody has a demon that drives them, that won't let them *not* create, you know. How many times did Cezanne paint that mountain? And his life was miserable. He had a tough time with his family but that was his happiness. It's a sort of negative thing with a lot of creative people.

I think we all look for some sort of distraction. But I remember one of my teachers saying that it was the fact that it was not knowing, not being restricted, therefore, that we got into what they call the Zen mind, where we just went ahead. We didn't know if we'd have enough money, we didn't know what we'd do, but we did know what we liked in a restaurant. We always hated to go out and they make you wait and go to the bar, you know, and obviously there's tables and all that bullshit. So we started on that basis. Anybody could come in and have a cup of coffee. But it was the unknowing mind, the non-conscious mind that we tapped into. It was not any preconceived idea, just going ahead and being sort of guided to do something that we'd like to do. That's my advice to people, really. You know, so many people have come up and made money now and they try to go at collecting art, try to find out who they think is going to be famous. Not because they're interested in the son-of-a-bitch's work, but because they want to make some money out of it. But I think in anything, including collecting art, just take what you like and the only gamble is if enough other people eventually like it, even if you want to just make money out of it. We hated perspiring Italian waiters and white tablecloths and all that shit and the icewater and bread they bring you, so we just said: steak and salads.

Why did you call it Nepenthe?

Lolly: Well, when we first started, this boy kept saying to me, what are you going to call this restaurant? And I said, "We'll call it the Log Cabin until I can figure it out." I said, "I'll know the name when I hear it." I hadn't figured it out yet. So he came with three pages of names and we went down the list and Nepenthe was there and right away Nepenthe hit me. See, I lived in Capri for six years and Norman Douglas wrote *South Wind and The Isle of Nepenthe*. That was the story of Capri only it wasn't called Capri, he called it Nepenthe. I thought, "Wow, there it is," and that upset everybody. There was more controversy over that name — you couldn't believe it. It was unusual. They didn't think anybody would know what the name was, and then people started looking it up. It created all kinds of interest. Beyond anything anybody dreamed. The word Nepenthe means surcease from sorrow, timelessness. Little did we know that Nepenthe was a drug, an Egyptian drug; but it's really a Greek term and it means surcease from sorrow, the isle of no care, and this place has had so many problems and so many things to work out, but it still is the isle of no care. People come here and they leave all their troubles behind. Amazing. It really works. People that need to get away from it all can just flop on the terrace and you can see what it does for them. People dance who haven't danced in years. □

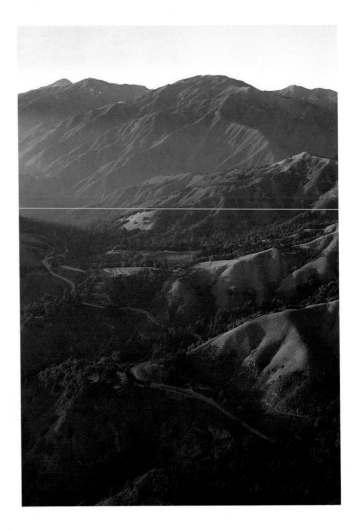

Looking north from Nepenthe (lower left) toward the Pfeiffer Big Sur State Park

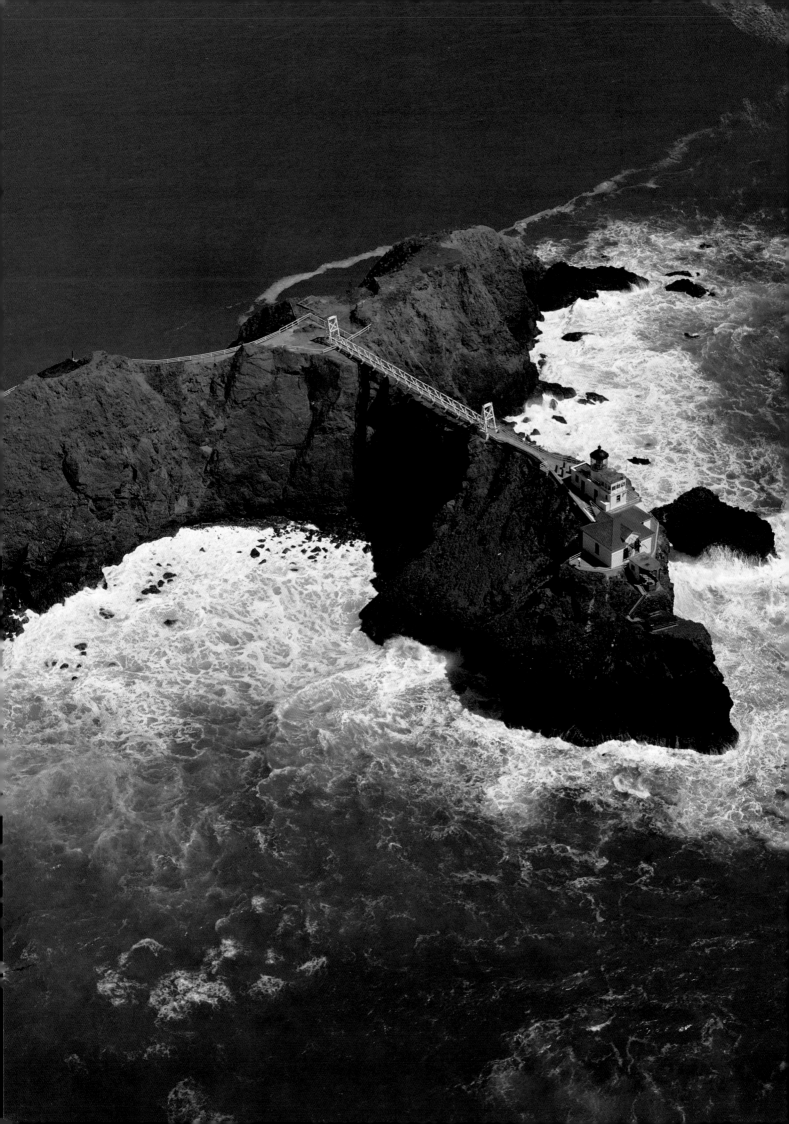

LAST LIGHTHOUSE KEEPER

Guy C. Sheets

When Guy Sheets, Coast Guard Machinery Technician Second Class, steps out the front door of his house and looks across the choppy, blue water toward San Francisco, his eyes take in one of the most astounding vistas in the Bay Area — a totally unobstructed, 180-degree wrap-around shot that includes, left to right, the Golden Gate Bridge, the tall buildings of downtown San Francisco, the sheer cliffs at Lands End, the Golden Gate itself, and the wide expanse of the open Pacific. On Sheets' side of the Bay, almost out of sight on the northern headland of the Golden Gate, stands a stately, Victorian, glass-topped tower, the Point Bonita Lighthouse. Sheets is the last Coast Guard Light Keeper on the West Coast — with not long to go himself. Point Bonita was scheduled to be automated three months after we spoke. A young, businesslike fellow, Sheets takes us down a narrow dirt trail toward the point, through a damp tunnel blasted into hard rock by Chinese workmen in 1880, and over a fragile, wooden suspension bridge swung high over a rocky inlet in which white surf crashes. The lighthouse itself, looking like a model of Art Nouveau architecture, is built up from a white base, with a graceful, 12-sided glass top set under a black, metal dome. Sheets unlocks a door and leads us up steep stairways into a bright, sun-warmed, glass-walled chamber, surrounded by the sea, and dominated by seven feet of tall, cylindrical, slightly curved and hypnotically faceted lead-crystal lens. At the focal center of the lens, a big, serious-looking lightbulb blinks on and off and on and off.

The Coast Guard used to be responsible for 16 manned lighthouses on the West Coast. This one, Point Bonita, was the first to go into operation, in 1855, and it's the last one to be automated. When they first built it, it was mounted way up there on top of the hill, but they had a problem with low clouds and fog obscuring the light — so in 1877 they moved it down here onto the point.

The lens is the original lens. It was ground by hand, in France, around 1850, at a cost of around $1500. It would cost $3.5 million to replace it today. It's all lead-crystal, hand-ground and polished. They use an electric light now, but originally they used coal-gas. They'd off-load coal on a little dock, haul it up the hill, burn it, pipe the gas off it into the lighthouse, and fire it again. A shield was raised and lowered by a clockwork mechanism to give it a characteristic on-and-off pattern.

The first fog signal was a 24-pounder cannon that an Army sergeant had to fire off every half hour, and since we average about 1000 hours of fog a year out here, that job got pretty old. The fog comes in and sits here for five days at a time, and he had to fire that thing every half hour. The next thing they used was a steam horn. The steam tanks are still here; we use 'em for air receivers. The steam horns were so loud they used to rattle the bricks in the wall. The air horns we use now are still pretty loud. If you're not paying attention and you get caught underneath 'em when they go off, you can *feel* the sound; the air and everything just vibrates.

When I first came here there were five people. They wanted you to maintain a constant watch over the point in case a boat got in trouble, and to turn on the fog horn. But the Coast Guard is short of men, so we're automating, like all the other lights, going to a more modern light and lens system, state-of-the-art electronic monitoring . . . and now I'm the only one left. There's a machine out there, a fog detector, and it turns on the horn when the fog gets thick. The only trouble is it was designed for the Autobahn in Germany, to turn on the sidelights when there's a ground fog, and our fog is a little different. The machine always turns on the horns when there's a fog, but sometimes, when the sun reflects off the water just right, the horns go on unexpectedly.

When they get the new light in it'll be even more efficient. Now I have to go down to the light once a week and spend three hours cleaning the lens and the outside windows because of the salt and the dust. If you leave it go for a week it gets really dusty. I've got a brush and a long pole for the outside windows, and I stand on the roof and do it. For the lens, I use glass cleaner and a soft cloth and go all over it. With the newer lights, like the kind we're putting in, you don't have to do that. Periodic washing of the outside glass is sufficient.

This light is an old design, using 1,000-watt bulbs, but on a clear night it has a visibility of 18 miles, thanks to the lens. As you can see, there are two bulbs in there, and if the one that's burning now fails, then the whole mechanism will turn around 180 degrees to put this other bulb right at the focus of the lens, and it will fire.

At the moment, this station is a decommissioned Coast Guard unit. Technically the Coast Guard owns it, but it's in a transition period between the Coast Guard and the Park Service. The main reason for the changeover is maintenance cost. The Coast Guard really doesn't have the money to maintain it all by itself, nor does the Park Service, so it's a kind of compromise. □

US Coast Guard Light Station, Point Bonita at the Golden Gate

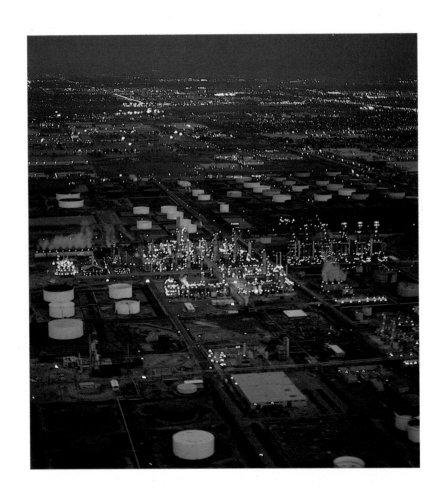

Mobil refinery, Torrance

Right: Loading coal in Basin Six, Port of Long Beach

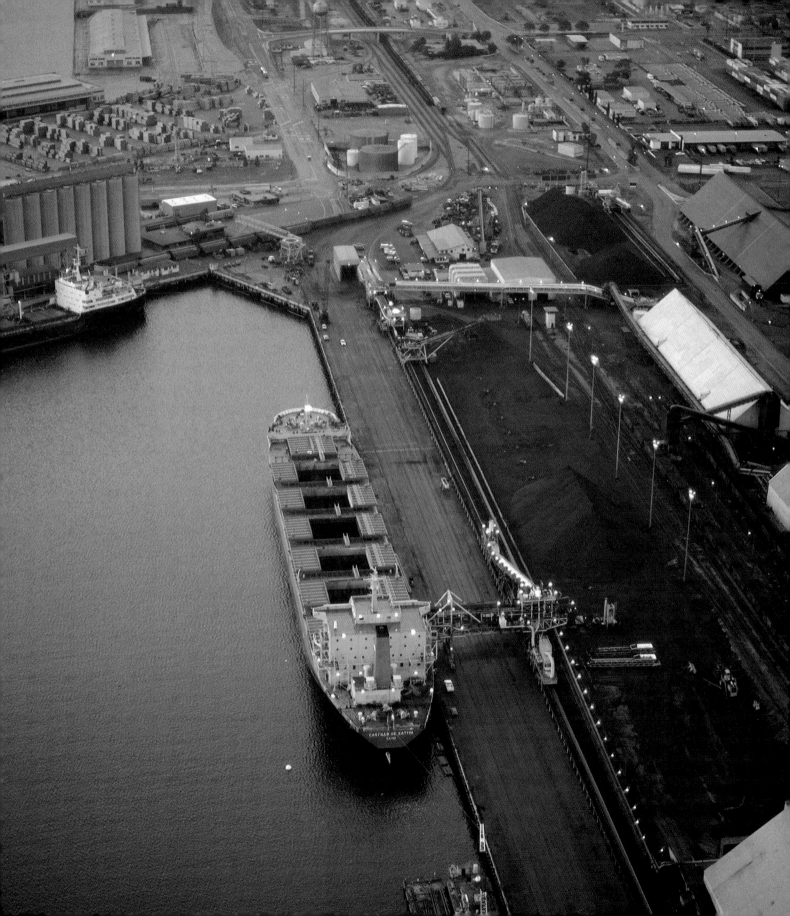

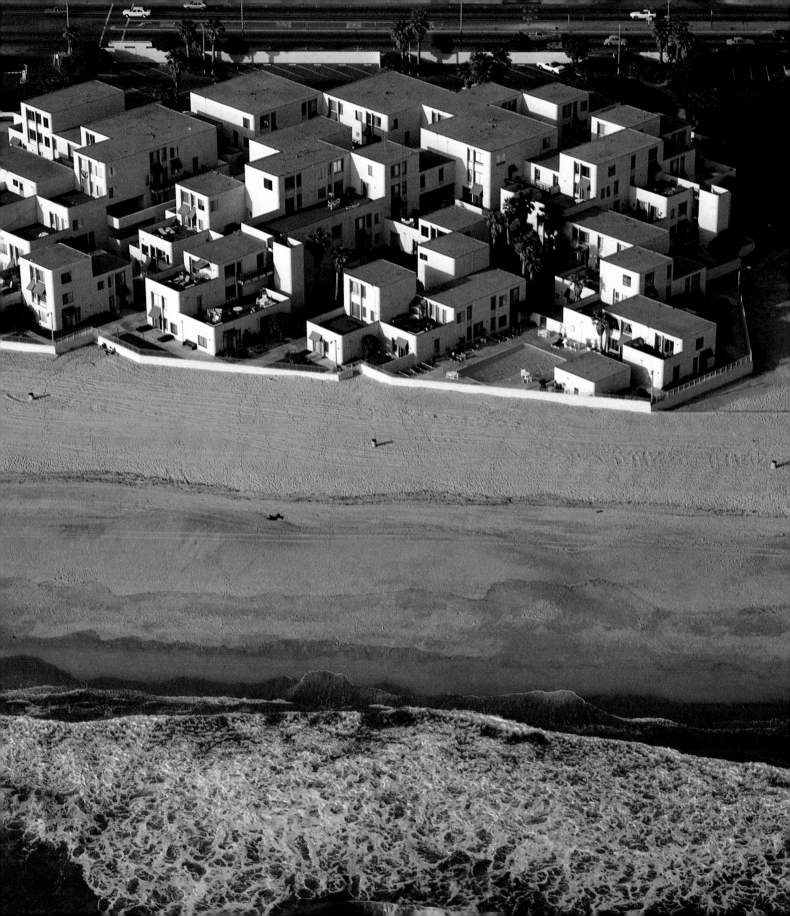

COASTAL COMMISSIONER

Melvin Lane

When California voters approved an initiative in 1972 to establish the California Coastal Zone Conservation Commission, all the political smart guys leaned back, nodded knowingly to each other and said, "Yup, the Commission is a flat-out, no-win job. Either the developers or the conservationists will cut 'em up, however much or little the Commission accomplishes." The smart guys were wrong. Dancing through a gauntlet of political and economic knives, the Commission assembled a staff, inventoried the state's coastal resources and established policies for analyzing zoning and development requests. Much of the credit for the Commission's success and longevity has gone to Mel Lane, who, with his brother, publishes Sunset *Magazine and* Sunset Books *in Menlo Park. Lane was chairman of the (San Francisco) Bay Conservation and Development Commission from 1965 to 1973. The BCDC was the model for the state-wide commission, and when it came time for Governor Ronald Reagan, a conservative Republican, to appoint someone to the state commission, he picked Lane. Lane's peers on the Commission elected him their first chairman. When Governor Jerry Brown, a sometimes liberal Democrat, took over the governor's chair, he reappointed Lane to the Commission, a post he held until resigning in 1977*

I got involved in all this because I was concerned about the economic stupidity of coastal mismanagement. Our resources are limited; if we consume them or abuse them, someday we'll have to tally up. Through my business, we were more aware of some things one would normally take for granted: the attractiveness of the coast, for example. People just like to live near the water; even if we don't need it for navigation or to drink or to dump waste in, there's some magical quality there. The ocean and the estuaries give a framework to our physical world.

Primarily, people came to the coast because of the necessity of navigation. And since land development has become such a tremendous thing in our economy in the West, the marketing system quickly told people they could get more for their house if it were on the coast, and that helped compound the pressures for development.

It's relatively easy to look at various pieces of the coast — a given species of plant or animals, the ecosystem of the marsh, land development or the natural state. But when you start putting it all together, you get trade-offs: there's no yardstick that works. How do you balance wanting to be free of OPEC oil against the damage done by energy facilities on the coast? Philosophically, you have to ask, what would you hope the coast to be a hundred years from now? That begins to give you some criteria of what you can do during the years until then. There are alternatives. There's a lot on the coast that doesn't need to be there. The big retail store or warehouse — they could be a mile back and it wouldn't make any difference to anybody. Or you could put a tremendous amount of residential development in, with coastal views and coastal access, without blocking most of the view to the coast or blocking public access. But the key factor is the *way* you do things.

When the BCDC got going, we found that when everybody sat down and looked at the same information, everyone would come out in the same place, even though there were great polarities in the beginning. When we showed them the facts of what was going to happen if you kept dumping raw sewage in the Bay, for example, the results were the same, regardless of who was reading them.

My job as chairman of the Coastal Commission was dealing with the process, not unlike my publishing business. Like publishing, I knew we had timetables to meet and we had to plan our efforts in pieces so we could get through the first pieces before going on to the last ones. Our principal job was not land use or construction permits; permits were a necessary evil and they got the press. But the real job was to study and analyze the use of coastal lands and water and determine what we thought should be done for them and how it should be done. But first we had to figure out what was there.

You wouldn't believe the number of people who told me it would be a disaster if I did this or didn't do that. But after a year or two, when I could see how things were working, I developed complete faith in the process. It works as long as you don't try to steer it to an exact destination. Half the time, I was just trying to keep someone from rigging the process. That's pretty standard, particularly in local government. You go to a hot city hall meeting and, in theory, they're discussing substance. But if one side sees they aren't getting what they want, they challenge the process, and if they see that isn't working, then they challenge personalities.

I was surprised there were so few attempts to leverage me through advertising in *Sunset*. We sell a lot of space to people with building products, public utilities and oil companies, which have great coastal interests. The big companies never gave us any trouble; it was

Huntington City Beach near Main Street, Huntington Beach, Orange County

the little two-bit developers that only bought an ad now and then.

I'm proud that we kept on target and we got things done and we raised the money from the legislature. In effect, it is the businessman's criteria. I was more concerned that everybody participated and nobody rigged the system. The process will go forever because as long as the coast doesn't get any bigger and you get more and more people wanting to live on the coast, the pressures are not going to lessen.

I don't think the threats to the coast are as great as they were five or ten years ago. The pressures are there from the economic interests, which want to use the coastal resources, but there's more counterbalance from the local governments. The biggest gain of the Coastal Commission is the dramatic change in viewpoint by people in local government. They used to rubber-stamp whatever developers wanted 10 or 12 years ago. They hadn't even thought about public access. They assumed it was some God-given right to do whatever they wanted with the shoreline.

Today, the local officials would say that when a man owns his land, he's entitled to make reasonable use of it, but he doesn't have the only voice in that plan. That's one of the benefits of having half the Commission members from local government. Democracy is probably the least efficient form of government — a committee of everybody. It doesn't produce the ideal answer everytime everywhere, but maybe there is no ideal answer. □

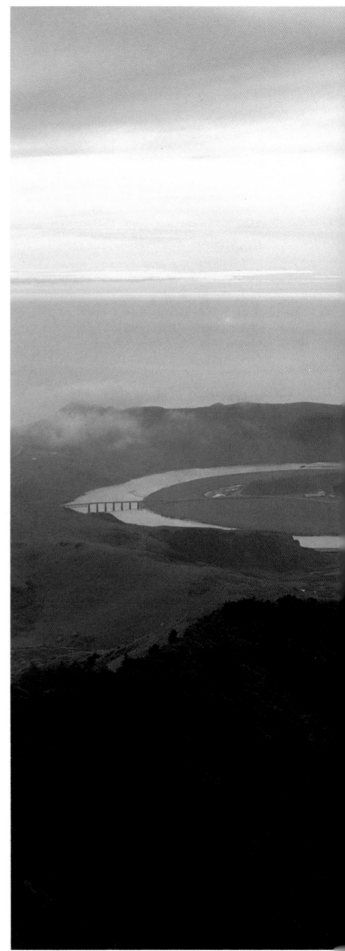

The Russian River meets the sea at Jenner, Sonoma County

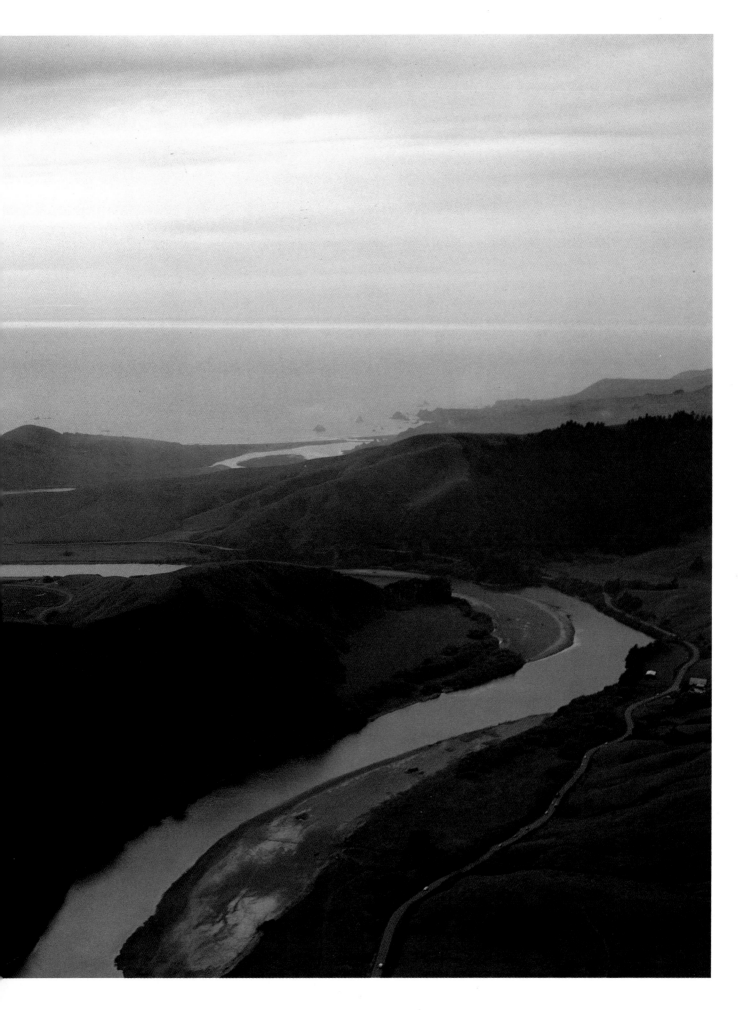

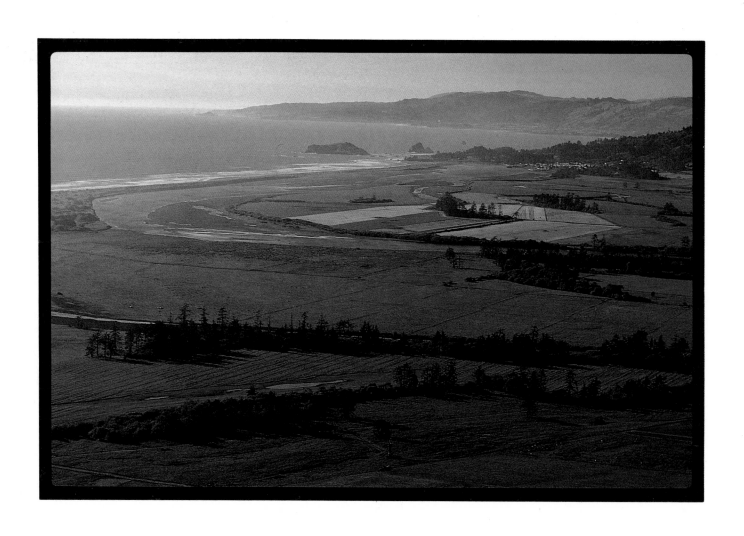

Smith River, the last town before the Oregon border

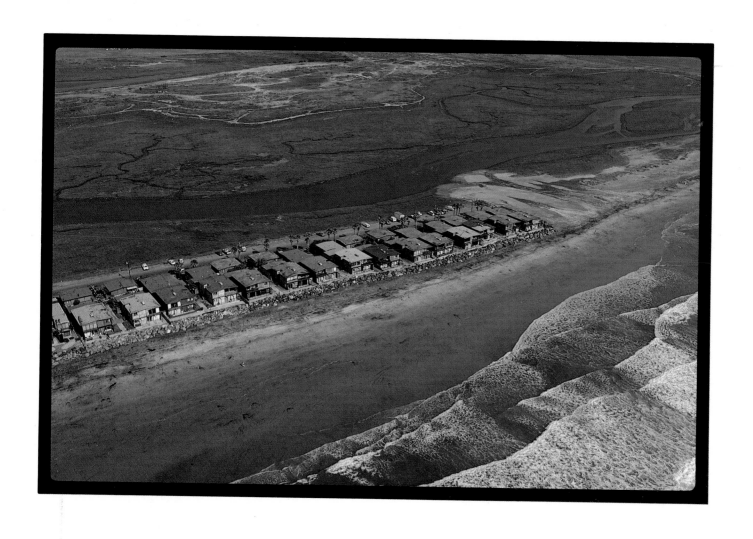

First Street, Imperial Beach, the last coast residence before the Mexican border

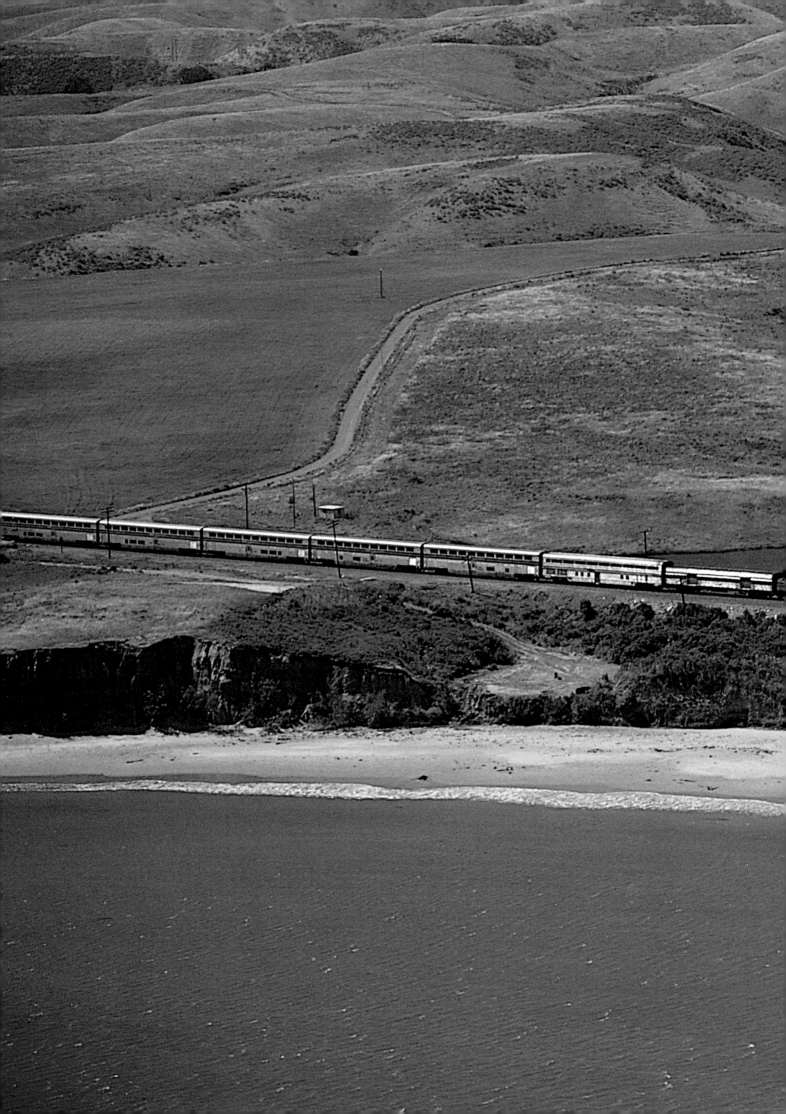

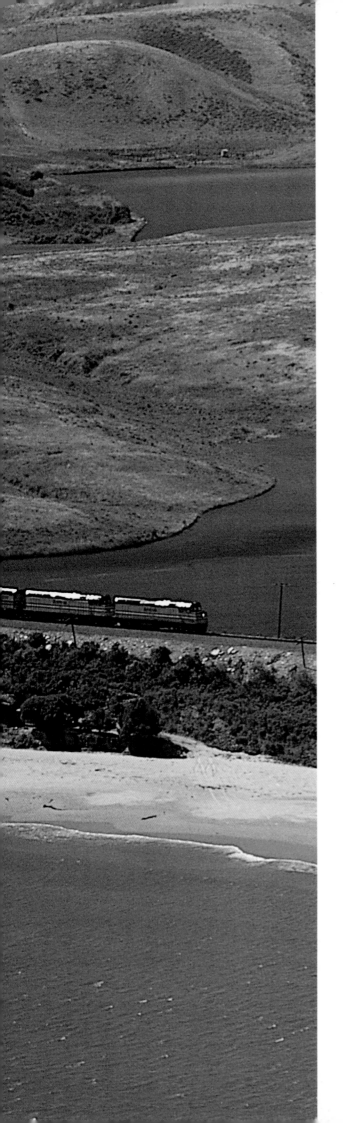

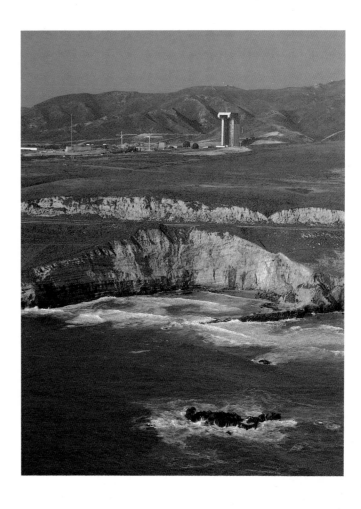

Space Shuttle polar orbit launch site under construction at Vandenberg Air Force Base

---

Left: Amtrak's Los Angeles bound Coast Starlight *near Point Conception, Santa Barbara County*

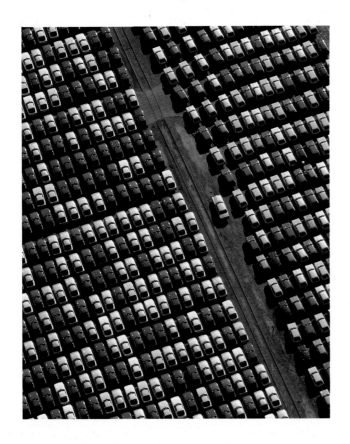

Imported cars at Port Hueneme near Oxnard, Ventura County

Right: Young vegetable plants under plastic in the Santa Maria Valley

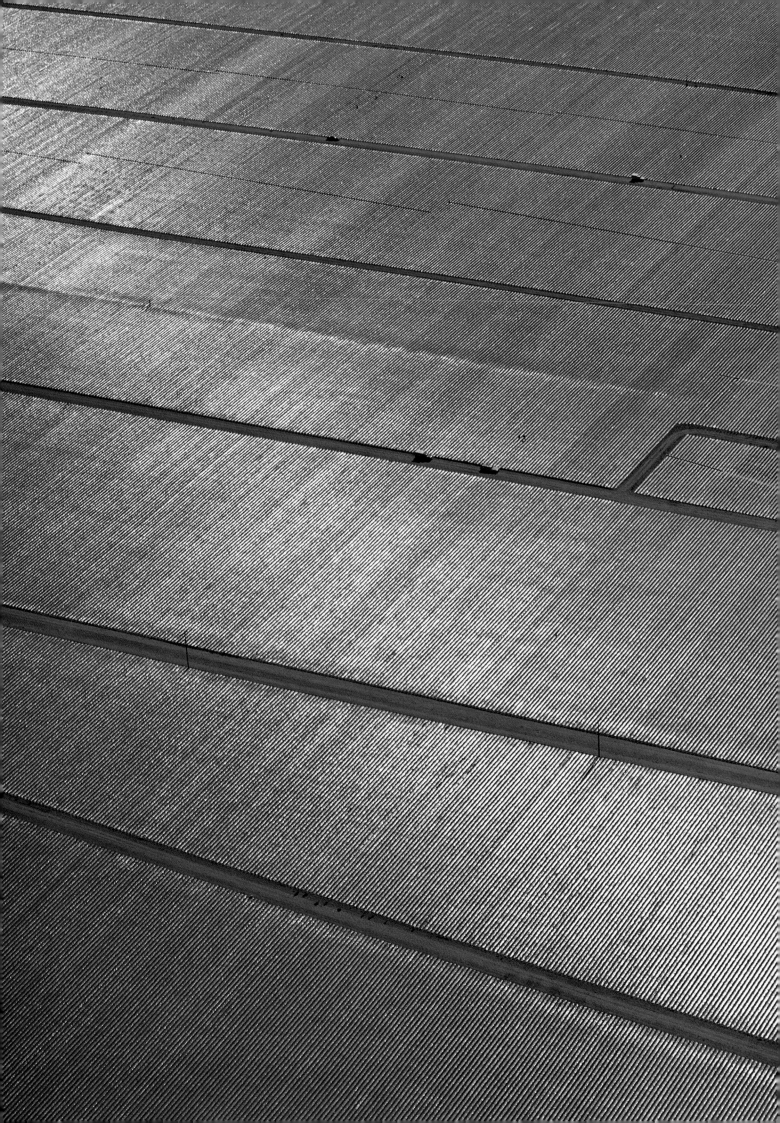

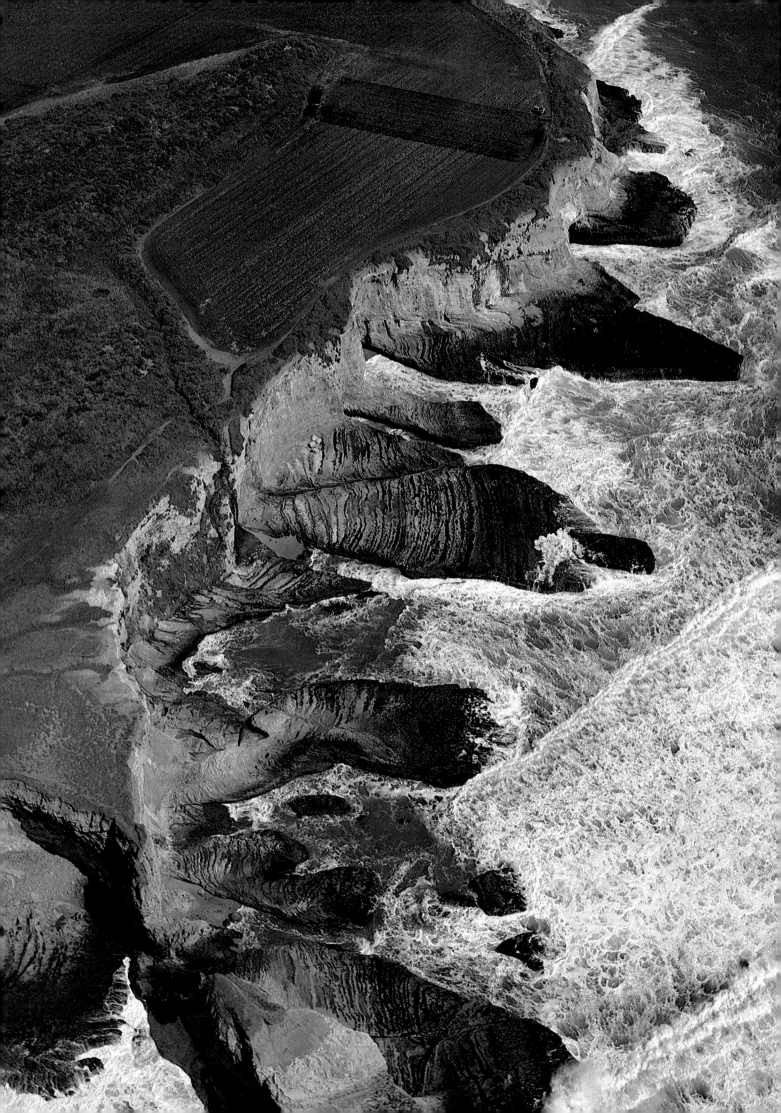

CITIZEN ENVIRONMENTALIST

Lenore Roberts

One of the citizen campaigners in the fight to establish the Coastal Commission was Lenore Roberts, of Portola Valley in San Mateo County. She eventually became an alternate representative to the Coastal Commission from her county. By the late '70s, her concerns were focusing on the loss of agricultural lands along the coast, as artichoke fields were threatened by driveways and patio bricks.

The meaning of "coast" depends on where you're from. In San Mateo County, it's a five-mile wide strip of land. But I grew up on a sheep ranch in Mendocino County. We would go to the coast for a day's outing. We would go over to visit Russian Gulch, where the blow hole is, to go fishing. So, for me, the "coast" is a little beach, a little cliff, a little fish. It's also sheep grazing. My orientation is land use, but the experience is total — the beach is not a beach without the ocean, the cliffs are not cliffs without the ocean. It's a wilderness, it's soothing, it's awesome. It gives you the sense of the vastness of the things you hope will never become cluttered up or spoiled. And it's constantly changing.

People who live in Wisconsin or someplace and have never seen the coast have a concept of the ocean and the knowledge that it's there, that they could go see it and that it remains unspoiled. That's very important. Recently, I was up north in Point Arena to a hearing on an oil drilling proposal, an on-shore well. It took six hours to drive there, and I was amazed at how inaccessible it was and how much that town had remained the same for 40 years. I was driving back at night. It was in the spring and the sheep pastures were all green, with the dark woods behind them. The moon was rising, a full moon, and the split rail fences and the cliffs and the water were all lit up as the fog started coming in. It was like being in another world entirely. And it hit me: "What would happen to this place if oil wells were allowed?"

When you look at which land is most available for urbanization, it is the flattest land, the land where the transportation systems have always existed; the oceans and rivers and railroads and highways. And that's the land where, historically, people and their agricultural products have been. We should recognize that the land is a finite resource, and as we convert the best crop lands to houses, we're going to have to pour more and more fertilizers and water onto the less productive land to maintain agricultural productivity. From a land-use planning standpoint, we should stop the encroachment of cities onto the agricultural lands.

If there were no more farms in San Mateo County we would first feel the economic loss. Then there's the loss of fresh produce near the existing urban area. And there's the visual quality of the land presently being farmed. In one's mind, knowing there are still farm lands — even if you don't see them — is important. It's part of the confidence people have in our country. If we were to suddenly lose our agricultural base, that confidence would suffer. In San Mateo County, something like 80 percent of the land in the coastal zone is owned by absentee landlords. The farming that goes on is by farmers who lease the lands.

The city of Half Moon Bay, for example, is right on the coastal terrace. Seventy-five percent of the city's economy is based on agriculture. But years ago the city limits were extended to include a huge area: they envisioned a city of 60,000 people. There are presently 7,000 people in Half Moon Bay. The City Council there doesn't like the Coastal Commission or anybody else telling them what to do. But it's hard to tell if that's a reflection of the people in the city. The dominant voice for so long has been from people who would like to promote development. In Half Moon Bay now you have people saying, "We can't live next door to this farmer who sprays his crops, so let's build more houses so we don't have these poisonous sprays next to us." Or the home owner's dogs go out and tear up the crops or their kids pick the crops in the field — all kinds of conflict.

Artichokes, Brussels sprouts, peas are grown. Some years, when the water supply is good, they grow some celery. In drought years, they grow pinto beans, wheat, barley. There are even some kiwi fruit and pick-it-yourself olallieberries — they're a cross between boysenberries and blackberries. Agriculture has not diminished its productivity in the county. Over the years, there has been some loss of acres in the coastal area, but it's still very healthy economically.

There has been a division over water between the farmers and the conservationists because years ago there was a huge dam proposed in a place that was a park or was becoming a park. It was viewed at the time by conservationists as a means for a vast amount of land development — it almost required it in order to pay for the dam. I now think there should be more cooperation between the farmers and conservationists to build a support system necessary for the agricultural needs of the area. There's a conflict between environmental groups who have concentrated on protection of significant resources, and the concerns of local residents. We need to recognize that both should be considered in urban areas. □

Coastal farming in southern San Mateo County

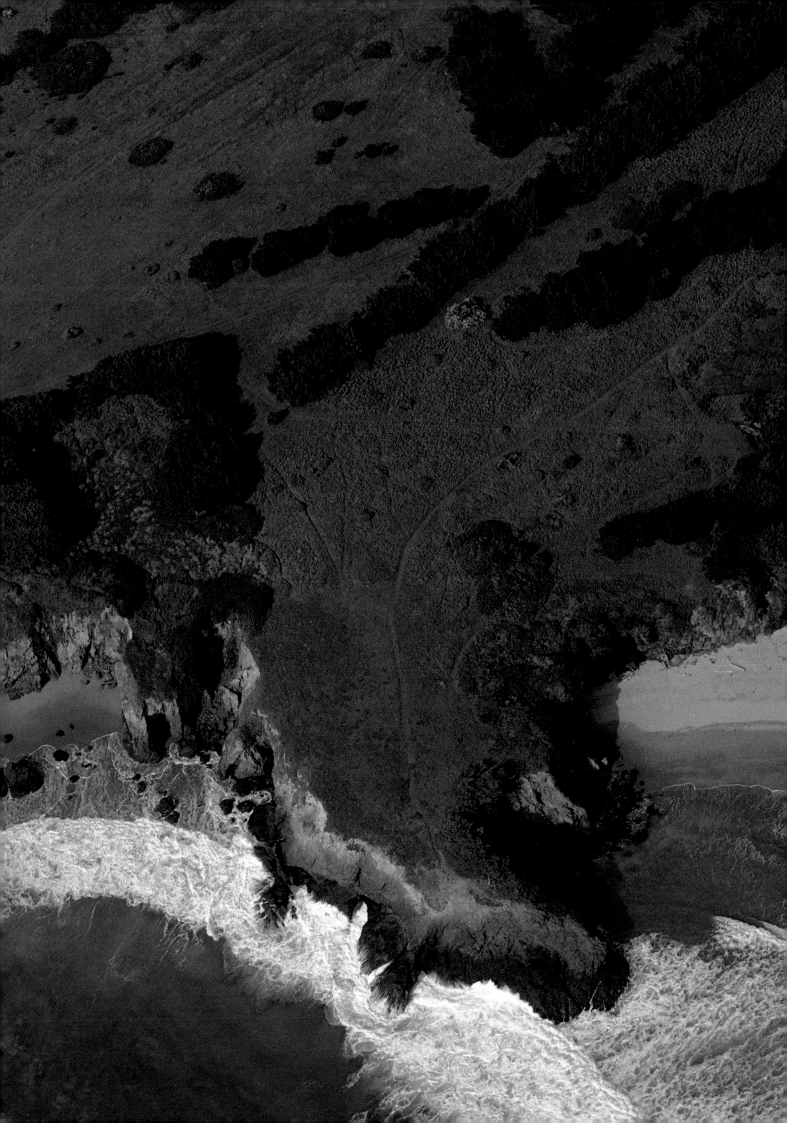

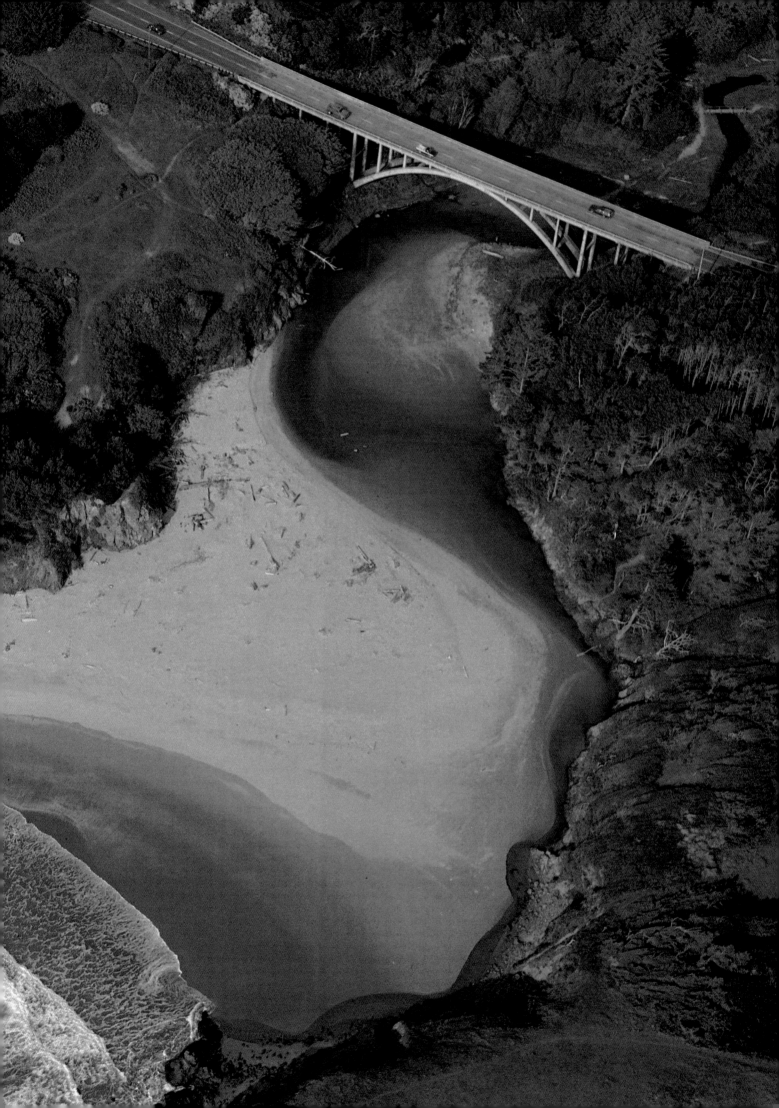

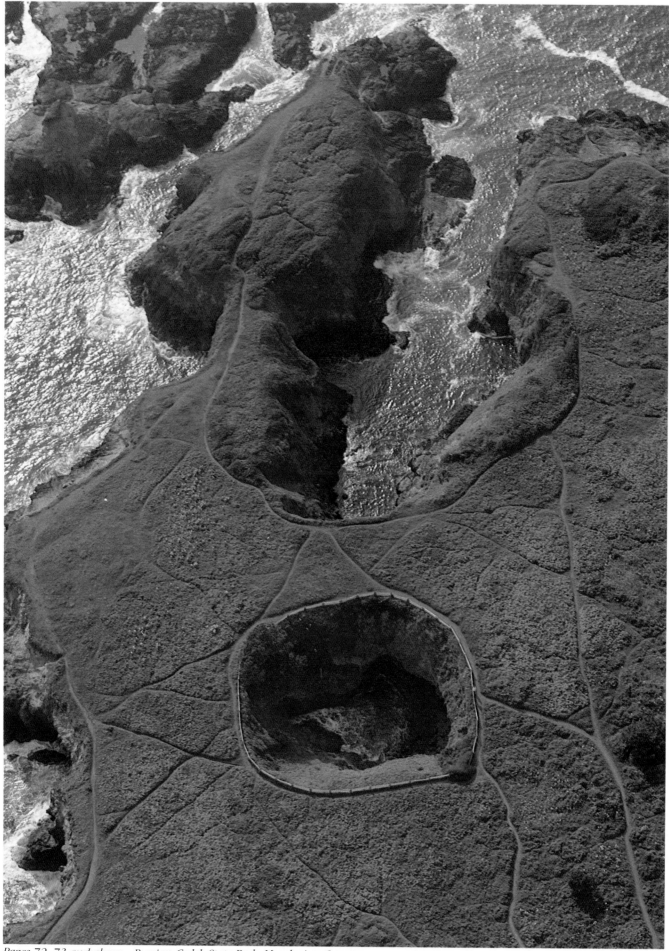

Pages 72, 73 and above : Russian Gulch State Park, Mendocino County.

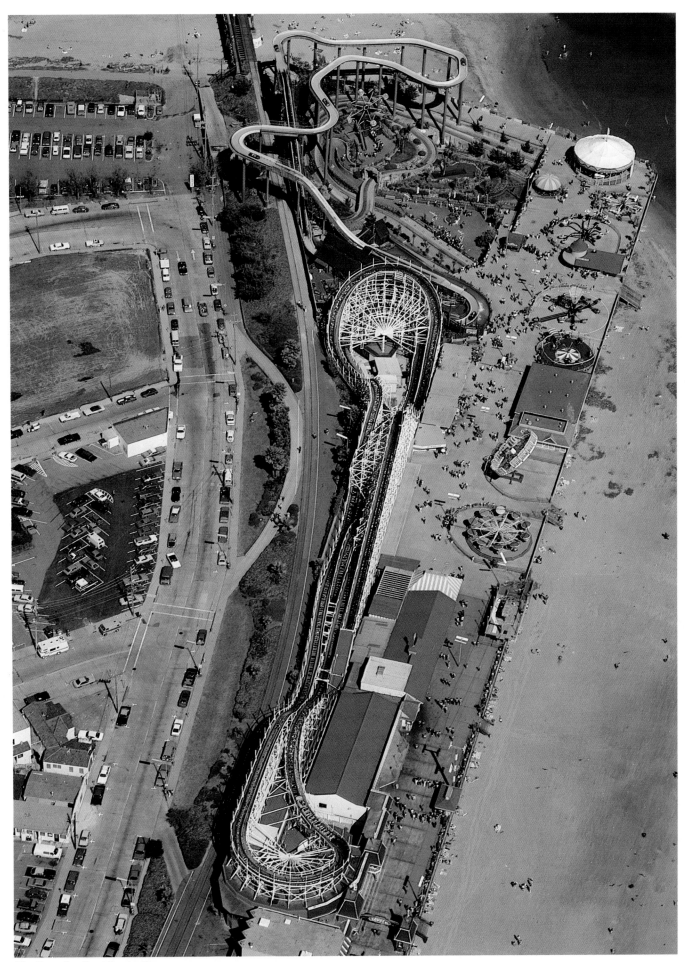

The Boardwalk at Santa Cruz

Right: Near Arcata, Humboldt County

Crops and homes, Oxnard

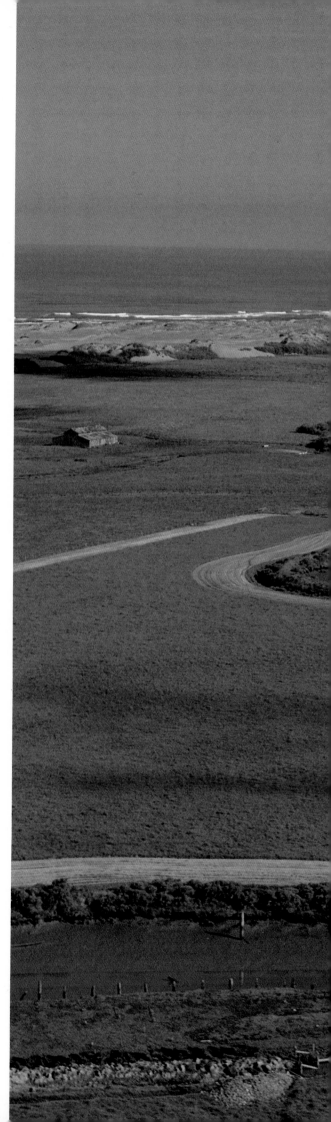

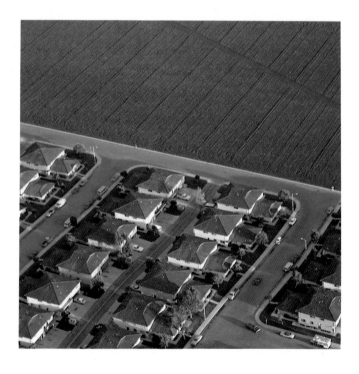

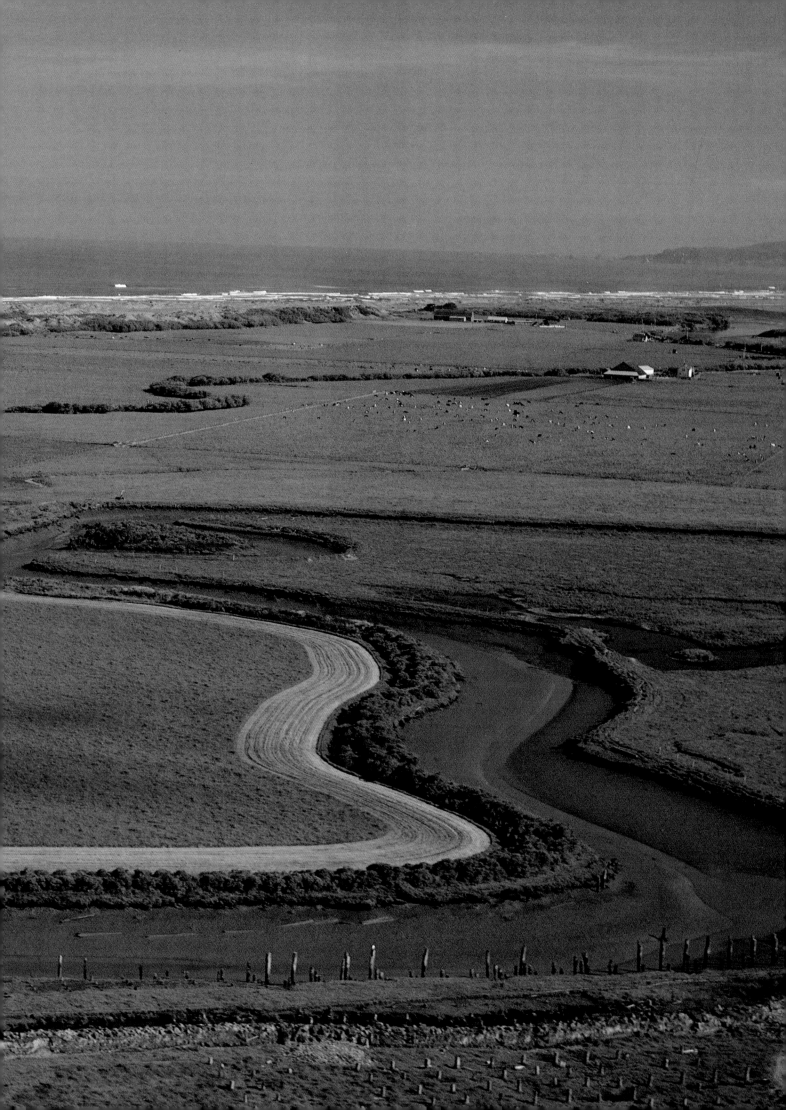

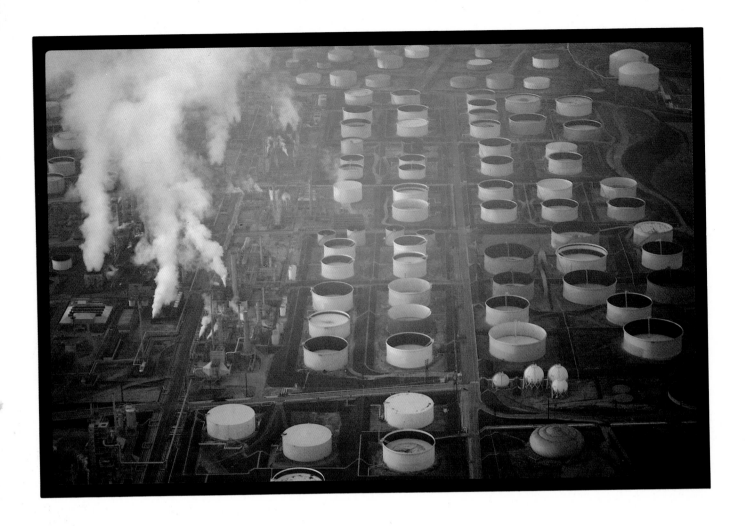

Union 76 refinery, San Pedro

Oil platform, Carpinteria, Santa Barbara County

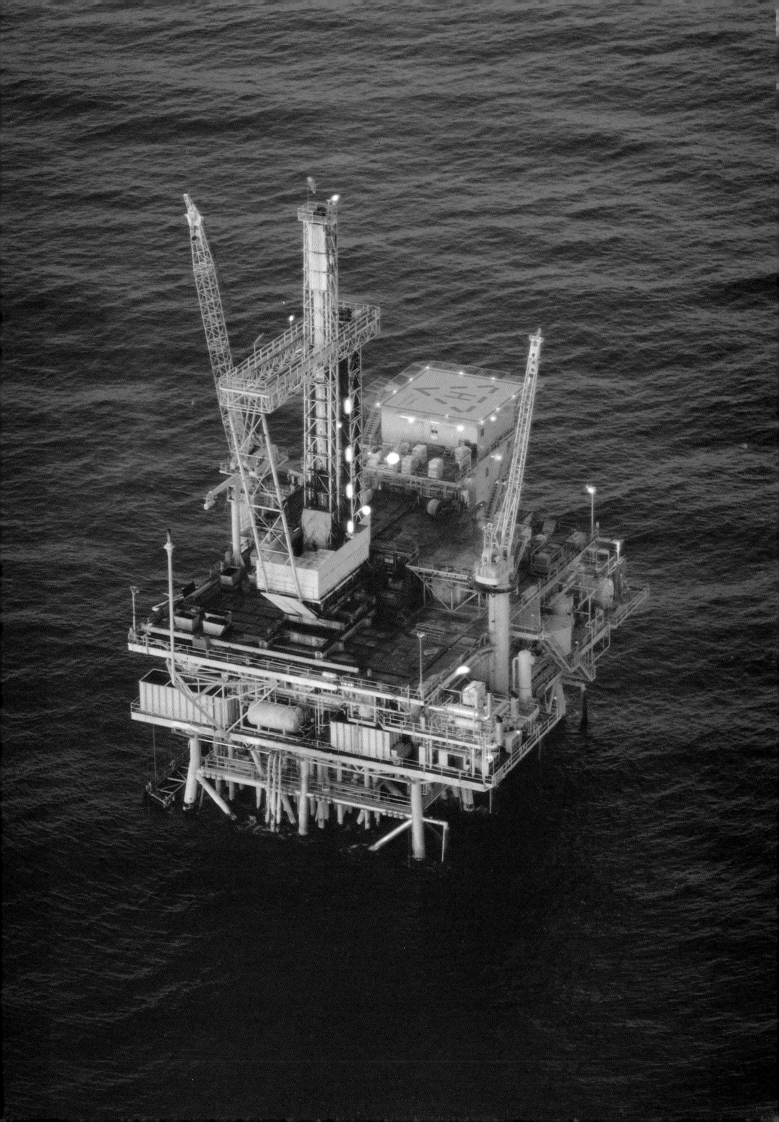

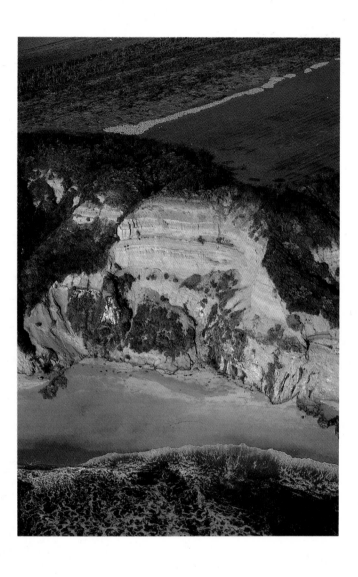

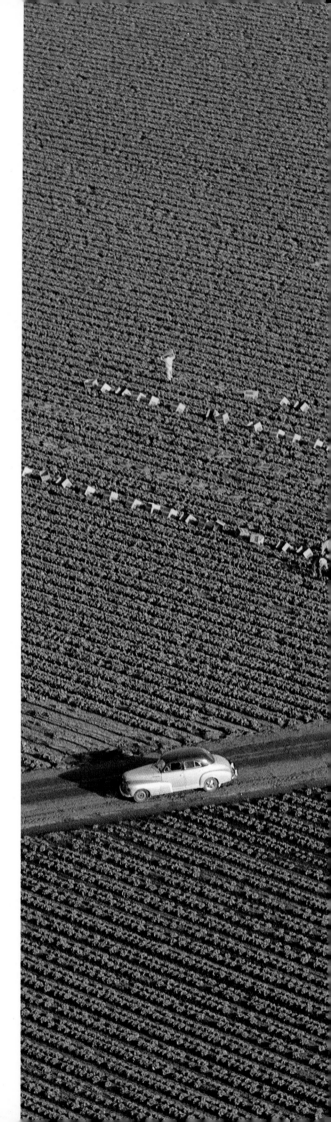

Pumpkins ready for market, Half Moon Bay, San Mateo County

Right: Vegetable harvest in the Santa Maria Valley

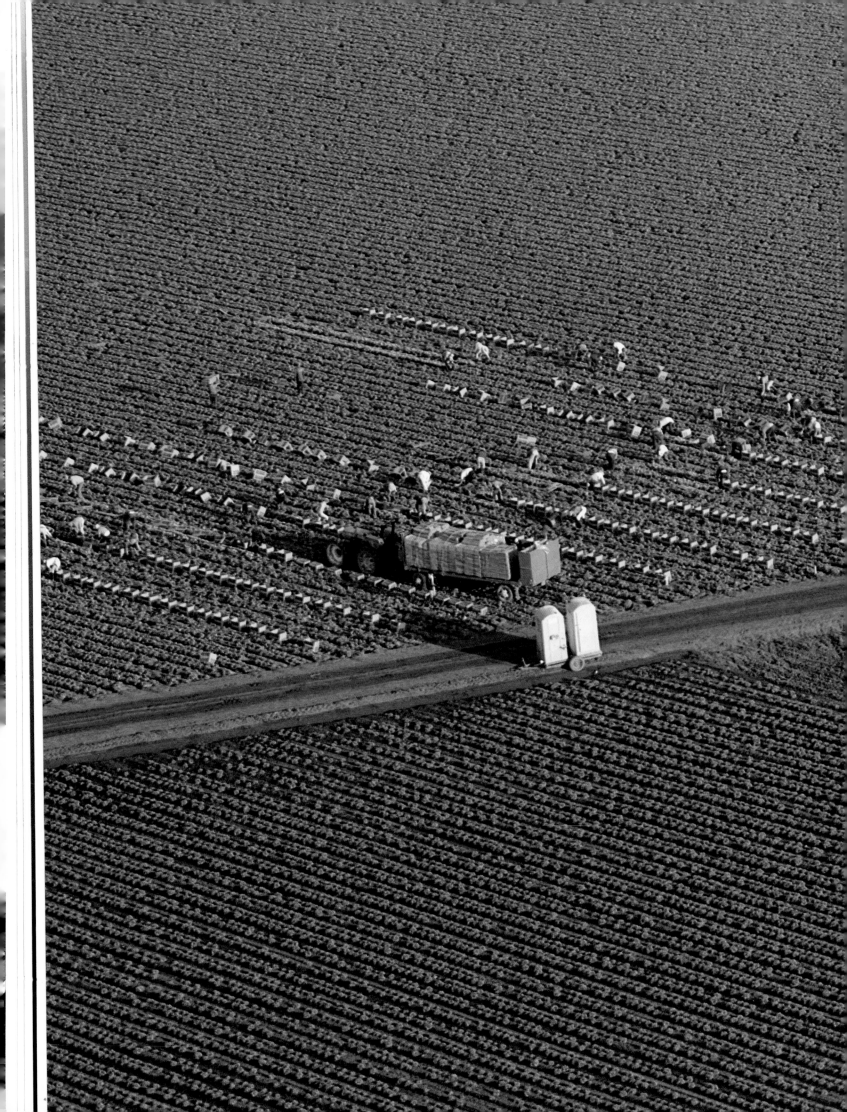

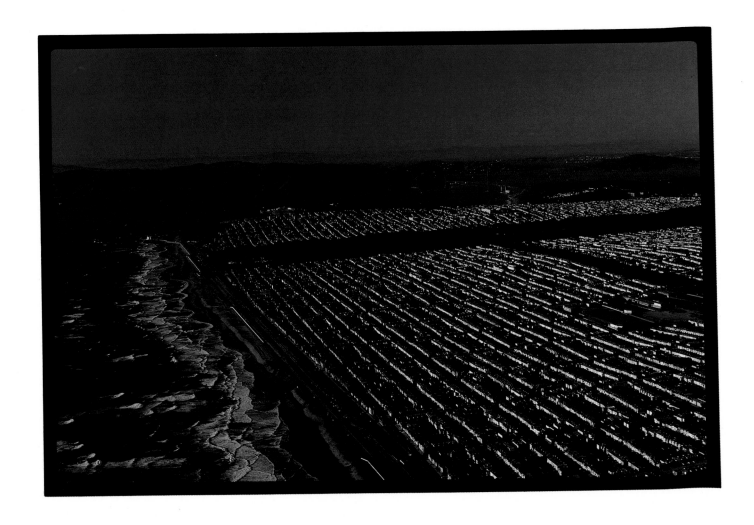

San Francisco

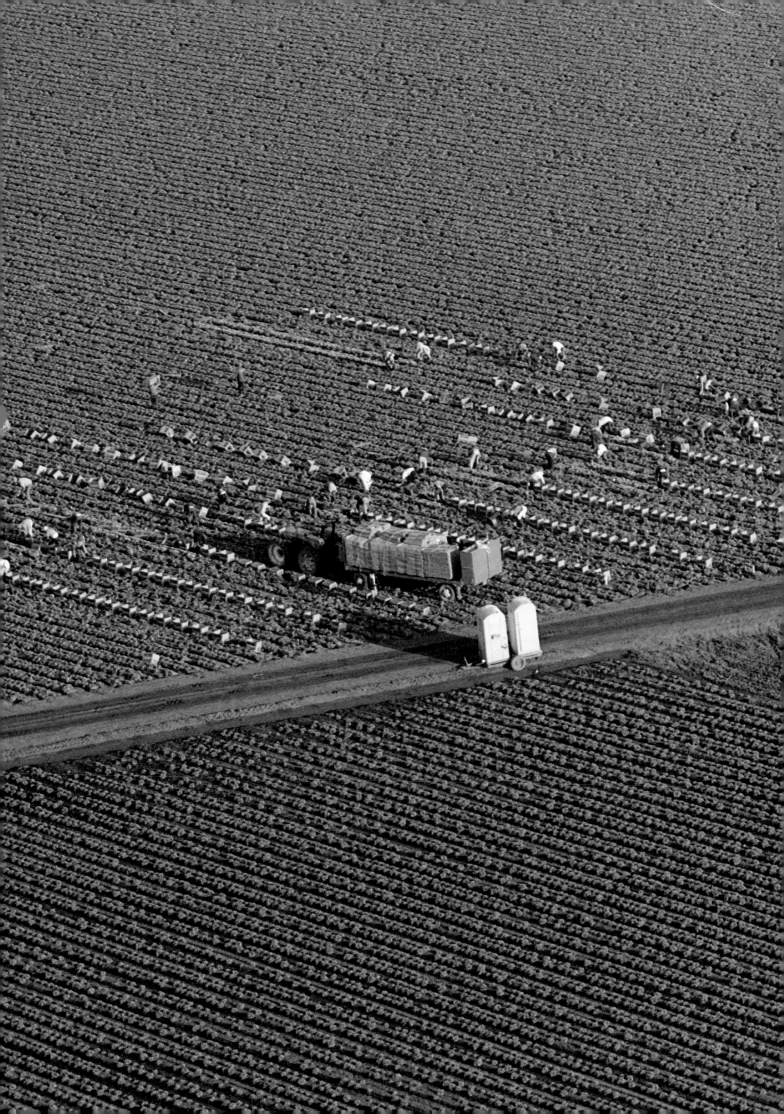

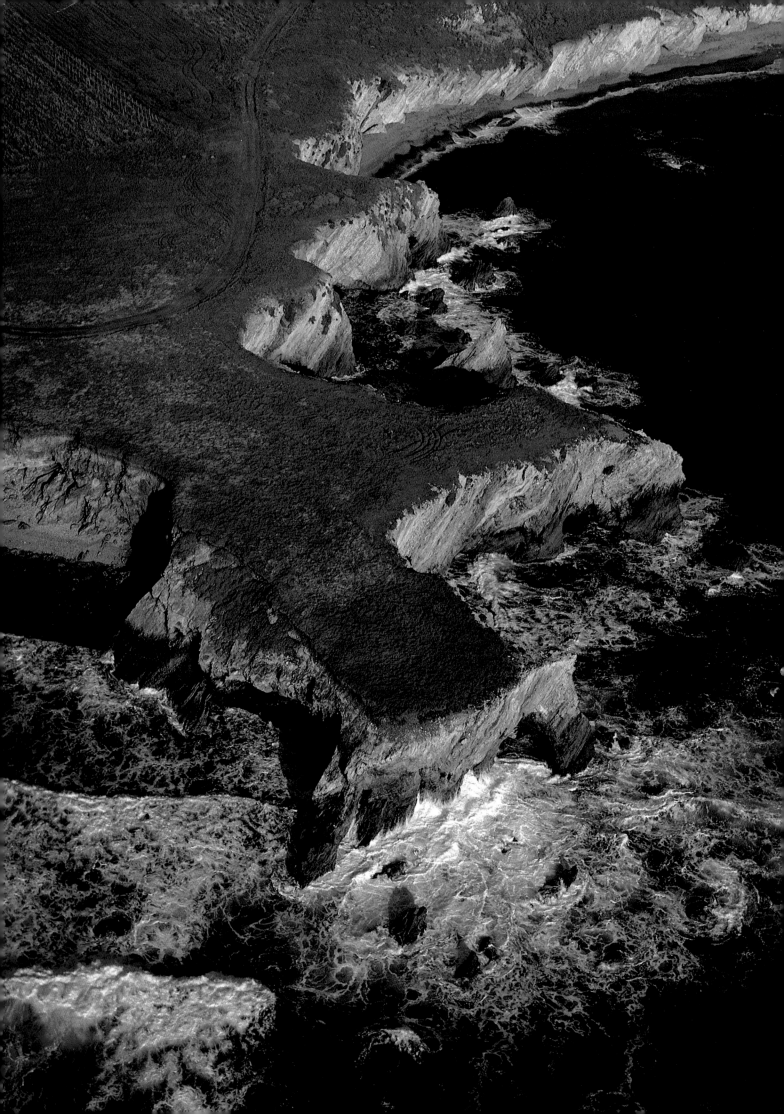

GEOLOGY OF THE COAST

Kenneth Lajoie

His office is hung with charts depicting the implacable upheaval of the earth's surface. For Kenneth Lajoie, a geologist with the US Geological Survey, there's genuine drama in the play of seismic and climatic forces and their impact on the coast.

The coast, as we see it today, all the coastal land forms, the beaches, the cliffs, the sand dunes, are only 5,000 years of age or younger. About 18,000 years ago the ocean was about 300 feet lower than it is today and the coast line was about 30 miles west of where it is today. There was no San Francisco Bay and the beach as we know it was just an inland position. You would have to go to the Farallon Islands to get to the beach. The ocean was lower because there was a tremendous amount of ice — water stored on land as ice — during the last glacial period. As the world climate warmed up at the end of the last Ice Age, that ice stored on the continent began to melt and fill the oceans back up. So from about 15,000 years ago to about 5,000 years ago the ocean steadily rose and the coastline moved inland. About 5,000 or 6,000 years ago sea level stabilized roughly where it is today and all the coastal features that we see on the coast began forming. Wave erosion cut into the edge of the continent making sea cliffs, and the wave energy working on the rocks created sand, created beaches. Large rivers that were coming to the coast deposited their sediment near the present coastline where it is today to create our beaches. In Northern California, essentially we're in a sand-deficient environment — we don't have many beaches. In Southern California larger rivers reached the coast with a larger sand supply, so the beaches are bigger.

The coastline tends to be very dramatic here in that it's a very young coastline. The processes that have been forming the coast over the past 5,000 years are active today. We're not dealing with a stable coastal environment. We're dealing with a dynamic coastal environment. The type of coastline that we see in any given place is a function of many factors, the basic one being the type of rock that's exposed along a section of coast. If it's very soft, the waves can erode it easily and make very high cliffs. If it's very hard, no terraces are formed and the cliffs may not be as dramatic.

The coast is eroding today. Wherever we see vertical cliffs without vegetation we're confident that we're looking at the result of continual erosion of the sea cliffs by the waves. In a few places the coastline is actually building outward. That's where sediment is collecting. In most places the waves are cutting back into rates of less than a foot a year. In some areas where there's soft rocks and high cliffs we have measured erosion rates up to about three meters per year. And that's causing some problems. If the cliff is retreating through wave action at an average rate of about two feet per year, a house sitting 20 feet back from the edge of a cliff is going to be in trouble within 10 or 20 years.

On a longer term, sea level will probably drop again because we will be entering the next Ice Age. Shore history will repeat itself. We've seen the signal now for the past million years or so in the geologic record, and we can predict that essentially the same thing will happen again in the future. Climate will become colder, water will be stored on the continent as glaciers and ice, and the sea level will drop again. At that time — within the next 10,000 years — we can walk back out to the Farallon Islands, where the beach will be.

With the motion of tectonic plates, there's a spreading center now someplace under the Western United States. The entire Western United States, from the Wassach front to the coast, is being ripped apart. We're moving farther away from Denver all the time because of the spreading motion. The West Coast has been pushed up over this spreading center, causing formation of different types of faults. One of which is the San Andreas.

So the Coast is sitting on top of a spreading zone?

Well, we've been pushed past it. We're now on the other side of it. And the coast of California literally is moving away from the eastern part of the continent. Most of the earthquakes in the interior of Nevada indicate that; the types of faults that occur there are all the types that we call tensional.

We read in California newspapers over and over again this notion that the coast or perhaps the entire state is about to fall into the ocean. Does the fact that we are past the spreading center suggest that the coast of California might fall into the sea?

On many geological reconstructions done by very serious scientists, we can find reconstructions where California has — at some time in the future, millions of years — detached from the continental land mass itself. And that is a possibility; there's nothing to prove it at this point, but it wouldn't be outside the realm of possibility. At some time in the future a large chunk of the western United States might somehow separate from the eastern part of the United States. But it's not going to happen in our lifetime, it's not going to happen within the next ten million years. □

Near Point Buchon, south of Morro Bay

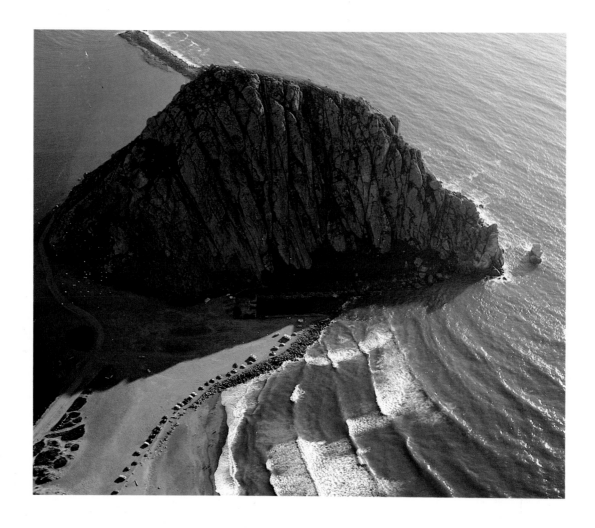

Morro Rock on Morro Bay in San Luis Obispo County

Right: Looking west to Morro Rock along the Los Osos Valley from 4,000 feet above San Luis Obispo

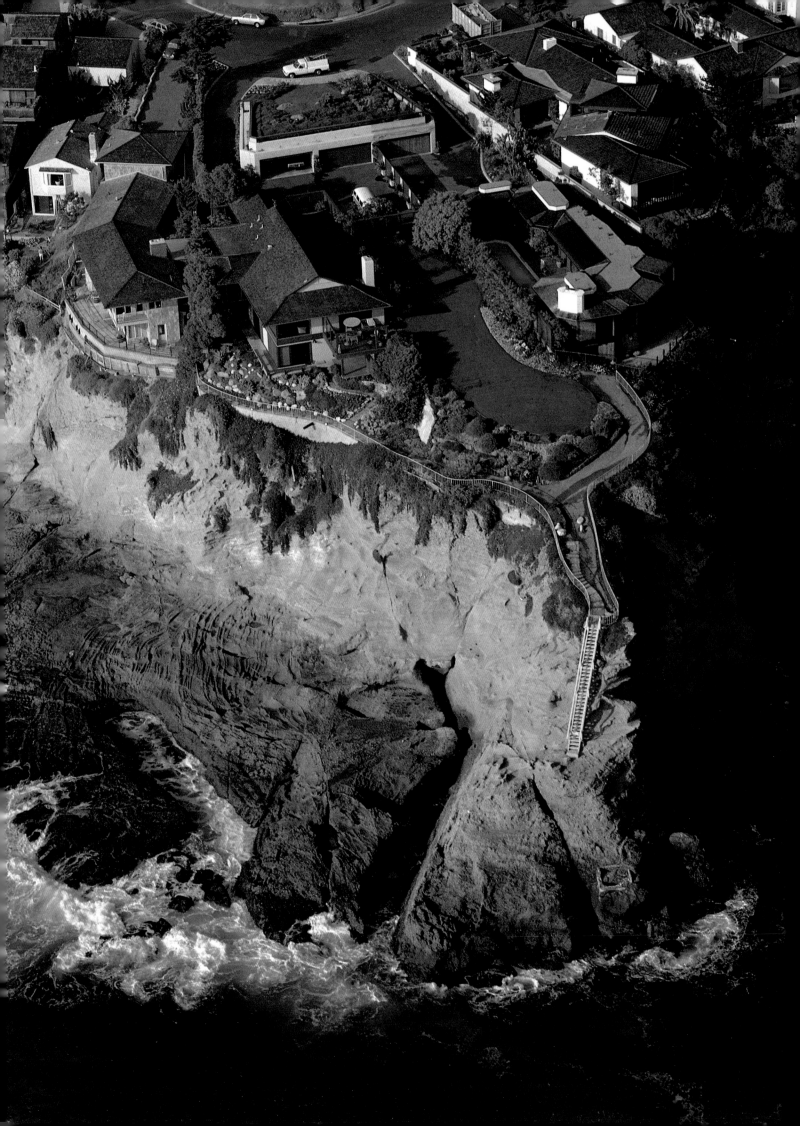

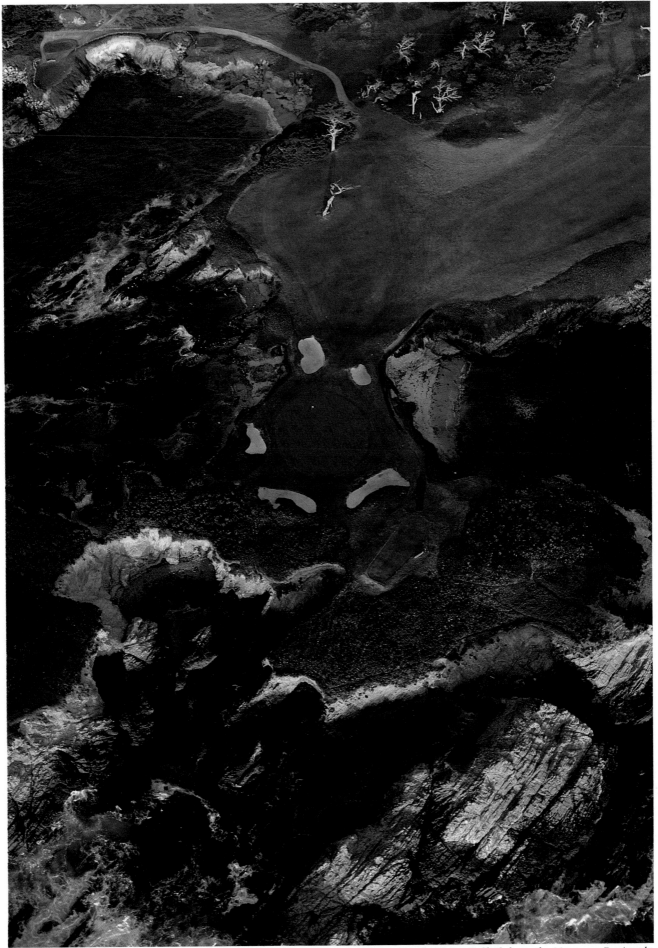

Left: Cliff dwellers near Laguna Beach   Above: The 16th green and 17th tee, Cypress Point Golf Club on the Monterey Peninsula

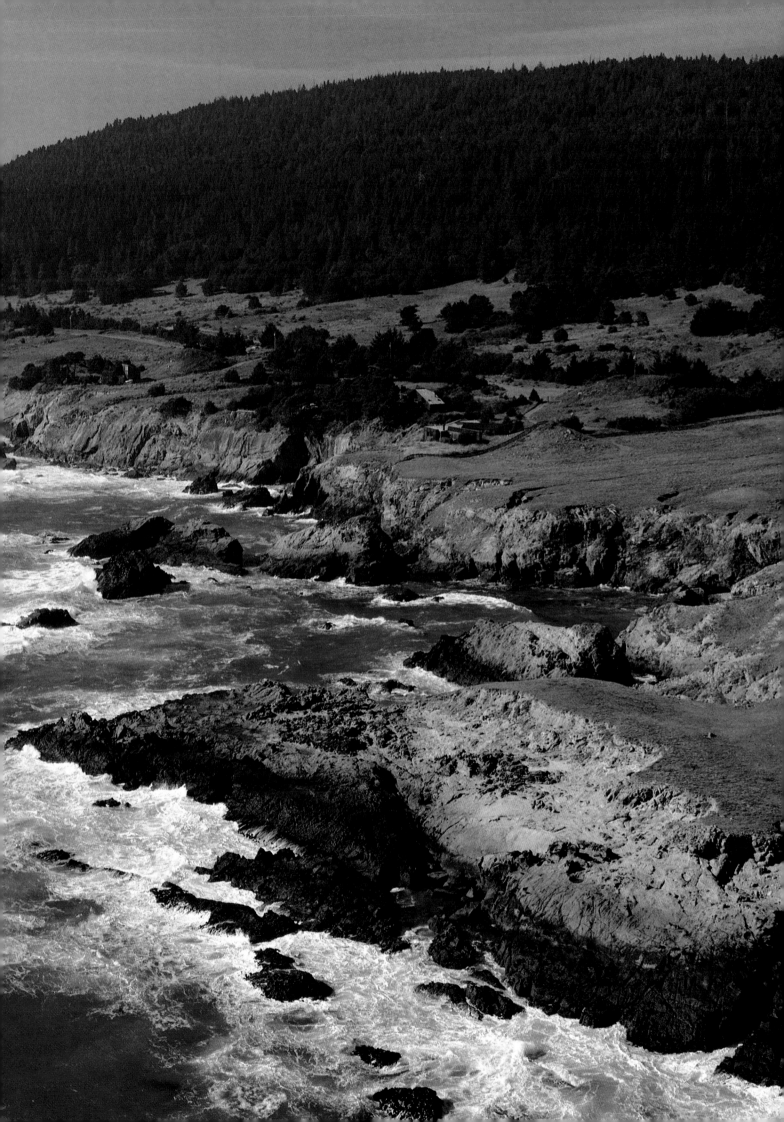

SEA RANCH ARCHITECT

Joseph Esherick

Chairman of the Department of Architecture at the University of California, Berkeley, Joe Esherick is one of the West's best regarded architects, with all the honors and awards that suggests. There's a refreshing plainspokenness about the man which is reflected in his work — and in particular the rolling, windswept coastal development 125 miles north of San Francisco called Sea Ranch. What's remarkable about Sea Ranch is the rightness of the selection of natural materials (including, especially, plenty of redwood) in that setting, and the marvelous placement of each living unit, affording to each great views of the coast and a sense of privacy. That Sea Ranch became a major political issue with the advent of the California Coastal Commission is, for Esherick, unfortunate — and somebody else's problem. At issue was the right of the general public to enjoy the entire coast, including portions privately owned. When Sea Ranch's developers refused to build the prescribed coastal access roads and make other allowances, the Commission ordered a halt to further construction there. A long and heated debate ensued: property rights vs. public access. Joe Esherick feels the matter has been badly handled all around. He'd far rather talk about creating an architecture to match the coastline.

It depends on which part of the coast we're talking about. One has to pay attention to the local environment. The buildings ought to reflect the nature of the strong winds that exist. The north coast, where the winds are really strong, is a very rugged environment; up north of San Francisco, like Sea Ranch. South of here the winds moderate a little, but not entirely. The coast around Santa Cruz is a little more benign, and down as far as San Luis Obispo and Torrey Pines things are a little calmer, milder and not as cold.

A building form that recognizes the fact that wind exists is a good thing — just look at the wind-swept trees. I don't mean that you should simply imitate the shape of the trees, but that the trees have automatically come to have the right shape, so it's a clue that you can use. Most of my experience is in the north. Since it is cold you have to be concerned not only about getting rid of the wind, which is uncomfortable and drives you nuts after a while, but to take advantage of what sun you get. There's lots of fog in the north, so when the sun comes out you want to

be able to enjoy it. Also a lot of the time the fog is pretty thin, so orienting a building in such a way that you can take advantage of the sun means that the building can more or less manage itself from an energy point of view. We've been working on these things for the last 40 years except that we didn't know we were supposed to be calling it passive solar. Paying attention to those things is extremely important.

Aesthetically, if you do things obviously wrong it creates a jarring note — if we put a replica of Mt. Vernon out there, everyone would know it wasn't the right thing to do. One has to be careful about the colors — there's a lot of color around the coast, but it's usually subtle color, color generated from wind-swept conditions: bleached wood, burned out grass, dried up by the wind; the greens are soft, not noisy; and the spray and moisture in the air softens everything down quite a bit. One should avoid sharply different colors. The California coast, culturally, has next to no relationship to a Greek Island — or the architecture of Greek houses. White-washed houses with white roofs are beautiful *there*, but if you transplant that to the California coast I think it's wrong.

The major technical problem to building along the coast in the north is that the wind blows like hell. When it's clear, it's very clear and dry; when it's wet, it's very wet; when it's foggy, it's foggy. The relative humidity changes enormously. The temperature swings wildly. There's a highly saline atmosphere from the spray that's kicked up, so you have to be very careful about corrosion problems. Any exposed wood has to be a lot thicker than it normally would, because it's just going to get worn away by the wind. Almost all the old barns that were built on the coast were built with split redwood planks and framing — extremely hard stuff and it weathers beautifully. Anything else is a problem. Aluminum windows popular today just pit and corrode, terribly difficult to keep them operating — you have to keep at it all the time, so the building is being worked on all the time. When you look at what Julia Morgan did on Asilomar it's discouraging because that work was done 50-60 years ago or more, and that's technically very well done work and very beautiful buildings at the same time. Asilomar isn't the most exposed location, but that's a great collection of buildings. The best work being done up and down the coast is being done by local craftsmen, like up in Mendocino. The old buildings in Mendocino, which is a very exposed place, were sensibly done. I've always heard that a lot of those buildings were built by people from the Maine coast who settled in those places, that being the nearest thing to Maine that they could find. Mendocino is a very well built little town. Incidentally, Mendocino is practically all white, but it looks wonderful. It's an acceptable

The Sea Ranch, northern Sonoma County

Victorian version of New England. There's an ordinary authenticity about Mendocino that makes it unpretentiously nice; it has a lot of the flavor of an Eastern seacoast town, but at the same time it's distinctively Mendocino.

What are your particularly favorite buildings on the Coast?

Several. Cannery Row in Monterey is great. We're working on the Monterey Bay Aquarium right now at Cannery Row; we're trying to build it back so it looks like an old cannery with all its industrial systems. Some of the old military installations are handsome. Fort Point, which was never used as a fort, is wonderful. The Kent family owns a beautiful group of buildings near Stinson Beach, called Steep Ravine: just a cluster of tiny cabins, what the New Zealanders call a "batch," which stands for a bachelor's quarters. Frank Lloyd Wright did a beautiful building right on the beach on Carmel; it has a copper roof, or enameled metal, which picks up the beautiful green color in the tide pools; it's a handsome house, sensitively done. I like all the lighthouses.

The condominium that Chuck Moore did at Sea Ranch is a very handsome building; there's a beautiful old barn just north of it that's wonderfully sited and tucked in and fits well. The condominium has a strong geometry contrasting with the rugged coastline; it doesn't pretend to be something organic, it doesn't pretend to fit. It gives a lot of privacy to people living very closely. It's a successful model — if you took that same space and spread it out all over the lot, there'd be all these diddly little dots around the place that would be unpleasant. We did six little houses in a cluster at Sea Ranch. They were designed together, which allows for paying attention to the individual nature of the views so that everybody can get the better views and sun without interfering with one another. There's a reasonable harmony in the shapes — they all respond to a fierce wind condition. In fact, we were supposed to demonstrate that it was possible to build a decent shelter there. Before the Sea Ranch, that country had a terrible reputation — you get blown flat the minute you open the door of your car — so we asked for the windiest location they could find. The immediate environment turned out very pleasant and the people there enjoy it.

There have been considerable legal complications over Sea Ranch. Did these present problems for you when you were planning it out?

Fortunately, I didn't run into many of the legal problems. The Sea Ranch was bought by a large developer from Hawaii, who — in the beginning — had great ideas about second homes which would eventually be populated by more permanent residents. They had a good planning team of Chuck Moore and myself and landscape architect Larry Halprin. We worked very closely together. We were perhaps more optimistic than was ultimately justified as to how the project could be developed. The idea of architectural control eventually got lost; they tended to do things more densely than they should have. But the development was carried out conscientiously, in terms of doing the best job one could. Sea Ranch drew an inordinate amount of attention from the Coastal Commission — it was singled out to be dealt with. I haven't paid much attention to the political wrangles; 20 years from now they will be sad-but-humorous events.

I do believe in responsible access to the shoreline by everybody. I don't think the coast should be walled off. I support the idea of access, but then somebody has to be around to police it and pick up the beer cans. The Fish & Game Commission has to police those areas so the abalone don't get depleted. However, I wouldn't support the idea of huge amounts of cars parked down in the meadow. If the place is going to be opened up, parking ought to be provided farther back so there's not a negative impact.

When you originally conceived the project, had you decided against access roads?

I certainly wasn't focusing on that. My view was that access ought to be provided but parking shouldn't be provided. One of the initial conflicts was that the real estate salesmen wanted the parking to be as near the beach as possible so they could drive somebody there and park and walk 25 feet, turn around and take the rest of the tour. Some of the motives were obscure. I'd hoped for local pressure to provide for policing, in the sense of policing the beer cans. The Sea Ranch developer was giving a large hunk of the property to the State for a state park up at the north end in a concentrated place; it was beautiful beach, probably the biggest beach on the Sea Ranch — goes all the way out to the point where the Gualala River comes out, so that in the summer when the river hasn't broken through, the beach actually extends all the way through to north of Gualala and crosses over the river mouth. On the land side, there was access to the Gualala River itself. That seems to me the most sensible way to get access to the beach — to try to claim that you have access to every inch of it, with ladders going down every cliff, seems to me to be absurd. The park is there now. But that apparently didn't satisfy the Coastal Commission.

To my mind, it's been an untidy battle; people can do better. That used to be heavily forested land up there; the landscape architect wanted a reforestation program with the original pine. But the Coastal Commission wanted to cut down the trees because you can't see the ocean from the highway. At the Sea Ranch are a couple of places where they used to load the lumber schooners down these little tiny coves. Check out *Ships of the Redwood Coast*, wonderful old photographs of what that countryside was like; spectacular photos of people riding up on these little platforms hundreds of feet in the air above the surf. But I never got involved in the legal wrangles — it would have taken too much energy. There are much more fundamental things to argue about — civil rights, et cetera — than somebody's view or access to the abalones. □

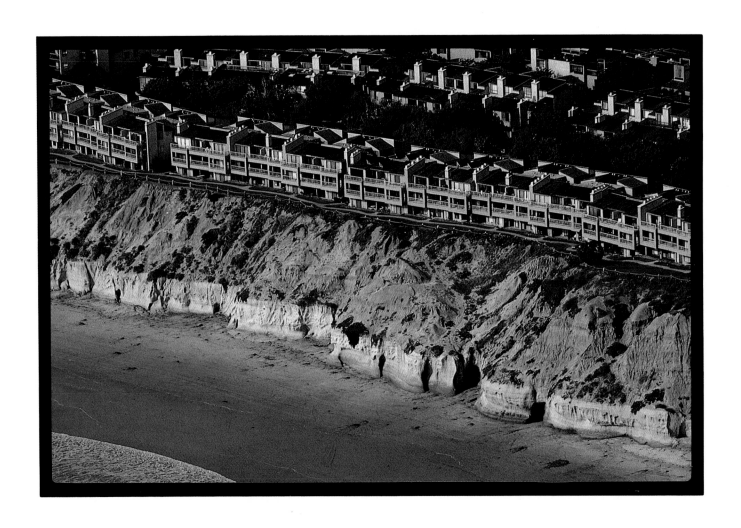

Condominiums near Del Mar, San Diego County

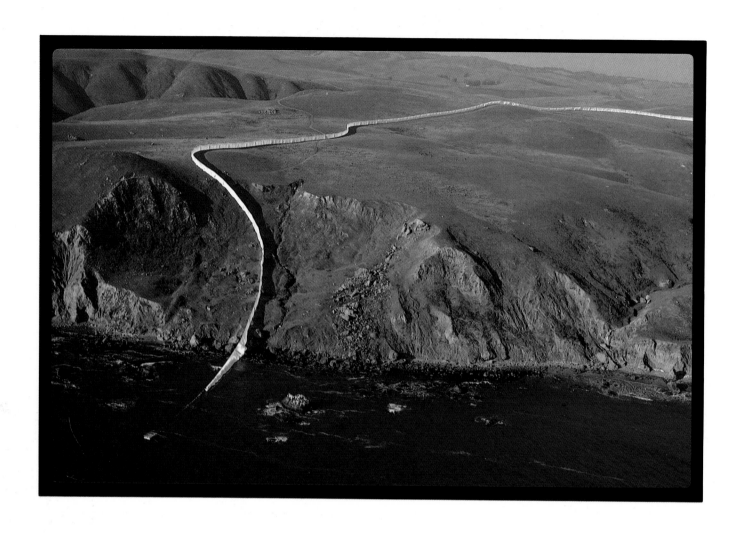

Christo's Running Fence *in Sonoma County, September, 1976 (Photo by Bruce Lauritzen)*

Right: Daly City, looking south toward Pacifica

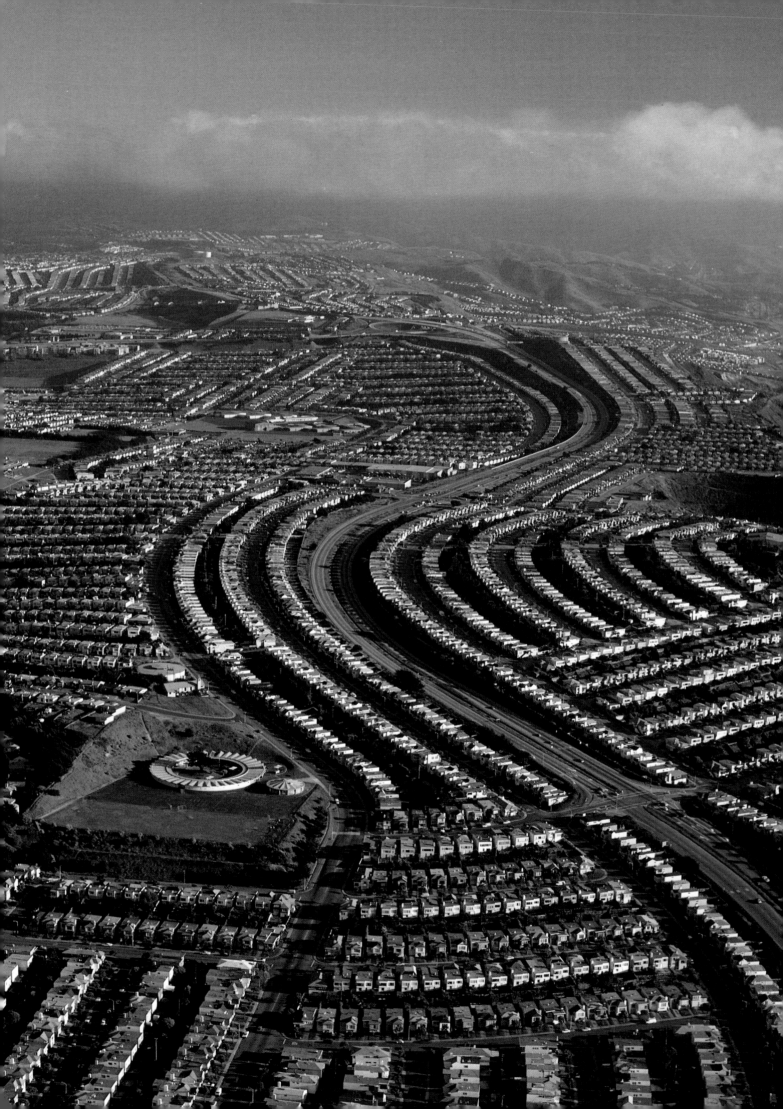

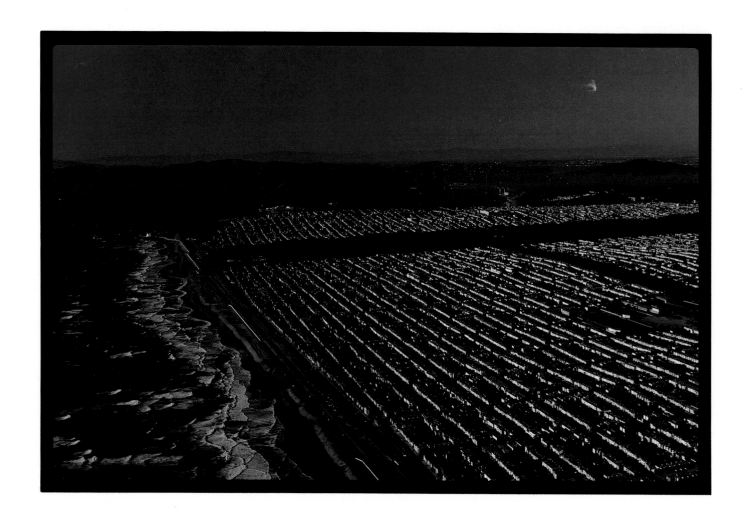

San Francisco

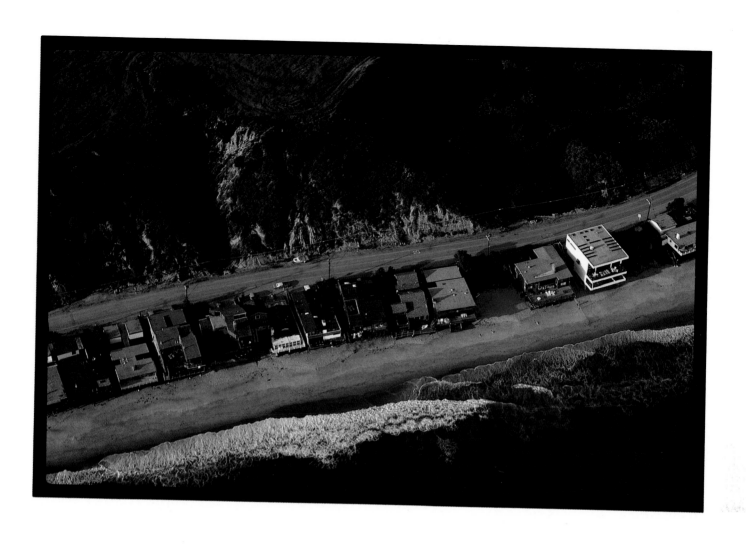

The "colony," Malibu Beach

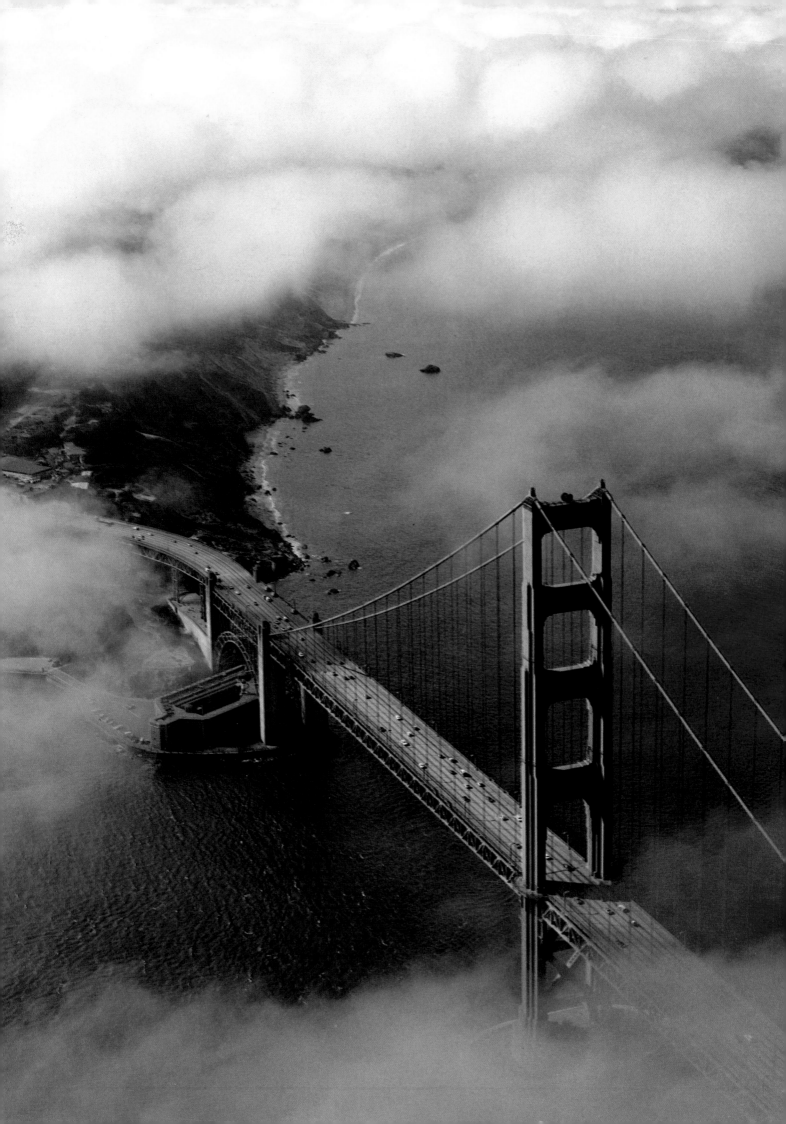

B A R   P I L O T

Captain John Weiss

When California was little more than a legend on the maps in Spain, ships were negotiating the treacherous bar into San Francisco Bay. It was the task of master seamen to meet the incoming ships and pilot them through the rough waters and over the barely submerged sand just beyond the Golden Gate. When the region matured to statehood, one of the first acts of its legislature was to formally establish the San Francisco Bar Pilots under the California Harbors and Navigation Code. The Bar Pilots, the oldest organization in continuous business in San Francisco, is a vital link for the city's maritime trade. Captain John Weiss (code name "Hotel") became one of 30 San Francisco bar pilots in 1976.

The bar is created when sand is dumped at the mouth of a river or bay. Out beyond Lands End you have a bar and this is where our name originated; the pilots bringing ships across the bar. There's a channel in the bar that's 400 or 500 yards wide and 57 feet deep. We can bring in ships with a maximum draft of 50 feet.

We go out approximately 10 miles beyond the Golden Gate Bridge to meet the ships. What's it like when you get on a ship? Well, it's getting the feel of the ship. You think about length, tonnage, horsepower, if it has any special characteristics, whether there's something that could go wrong. You think about what route you're going to take and the people you have to contact, the passing of other vessels, any kind of obstructions or other craft in the vicinity.

I graduated in 1963 from the California Maritime Academy and from there I went to work for Standard Oil as a ship's officer, primarily second and third mate. Then I worked for Hills Petroleum Company as chief mate and, later, a ship's master.

For the officer's license, you take about 36 hours of Coast Guard examinations. The pilot's license is the hardest license, about a 40-hour exam. After you have the license, you put in your application for appointment as a bar pilot. Then it's a matter of waiting for somebody to quit, retire or die.

We go to a ship at the dock and take it out. Outside the bar, we get off the bigger ship and get on our 85-foot pilot boat, the *California*. It's on-station out there all the time, so you get on the pilot boat and wait for the next ship that needs to be brought into port.

You get from the pilot boat to the incoming ship by going up the side on a Jacob's ladder. You get off the same way, depending on the sea conditions. Normally, you come part way down the ladder and then swing down on a three-and-one-half-inch line. If you come too far down the ladder, the pilot boat has a tendency to pitch up and catch you hard, so you usually leap down off the rope.

Bad weather and getting on and off the ship, that's the big problem. About one pilot a year goes in the water. We all wear life jackets, actually they're "float coats." They're not the heavy-duty, hypothermia suits; these just keep you afloat. In one pocket there's a strobe light so the pilot boat can find you at night and a safety line with a "D" ring that you can hook onto a recovery line.

Until 1973, we had a wooden schooner for a pilot boat and used 14-foot yawls to transfer the pilots, yawls with outboard motors. It was a much wetter operation, but there wasn't a 100-ton boat waiting below to crunch you between the hulls like there is now.

Sometimes, if the weather's real rough, a pilot gets stuck on the ship. Last year, we were doing some stability tests and I had two naval architects going out with me. The forecast was for moderating conditions outside the Golden Gate. By the time the ship reached the pilot boat, the weather hadn't moderated, it had really made up. I spent two days with the architects going to Los Angeles: there was no way to get off the ship.

The fog can be difficult. This morning coming in there was an old wooden Navy vessel ahead of us and it got under the bridge so the radar wasn't picking it up too well. So we made the turn and held a little high for him, but still, he was kinda close when we went past.

There are a lot of factors in the fog, but you have pretty good equipment in all the vessels now; most of them have pretty good radar sets. It's not like the olden days when they went strictly by whistle signals and sounding boards.

One big problem is the language barrier. Maybe you have a captain who knows a little English, but you can't understand him or he can't understand you. Other than that and the weather, it's pretty cut and dried. There's an art to it, but nothing scientific about it. You have to get your thoughts across to these people. If you can't accomplish that, then you've got some problems.

Some people like to work during the day, but I like night best. For one thing, it's easier to distinguish lights and stuff. Also, you don't have the traffic that you have during daytime — small boats, that type of thing. I just like the feeling at night; it's a personal preference.

It's an interesting job. I think it's the best in the whole maritime industry. The average pilot stays here about 17 or 18 years. You've got to remember that pilots, when they come here, already have been serving as ship's masters, so this becomes the culmination of an already successful career. □

The Golden Gate Bridge

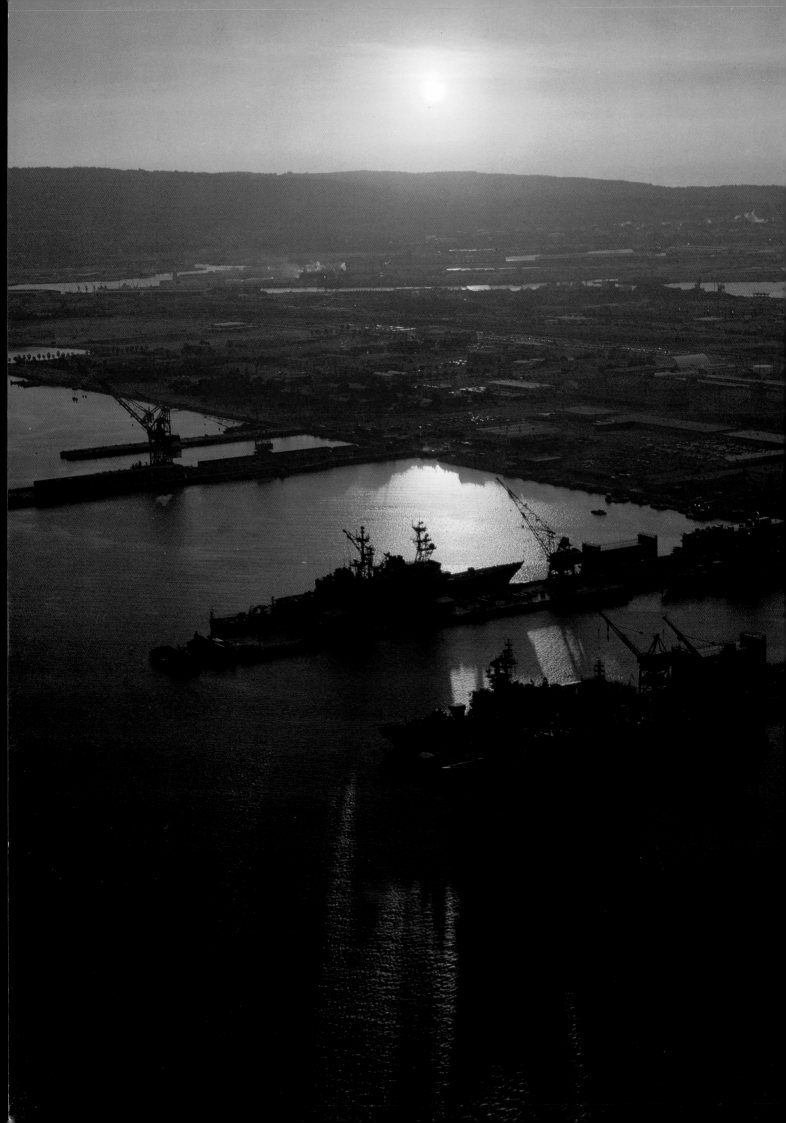

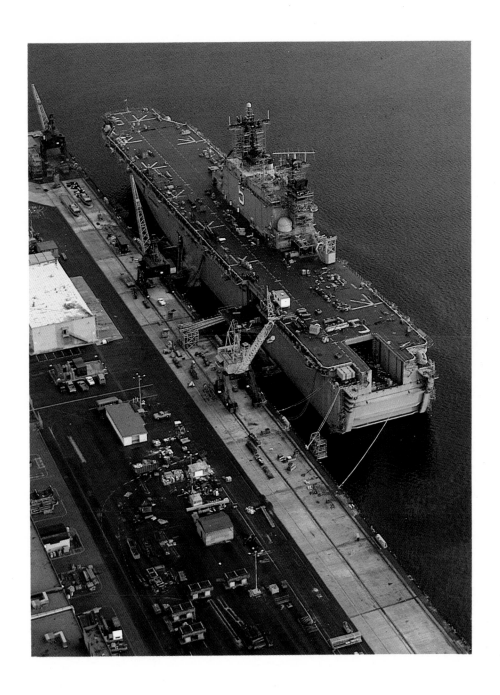

At work on an attack carrier, Long Beach Naval Shipyard

Left: The Palos Verdes Hills beyond the Long Beach Naval Shipyard

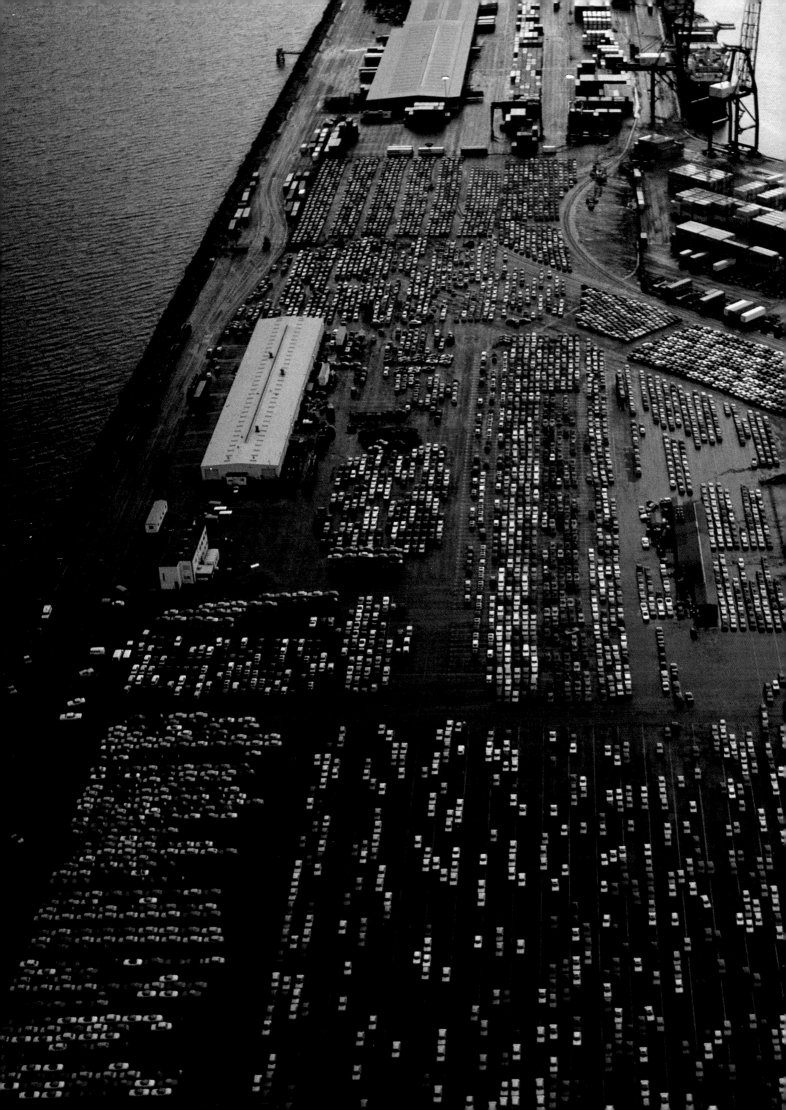

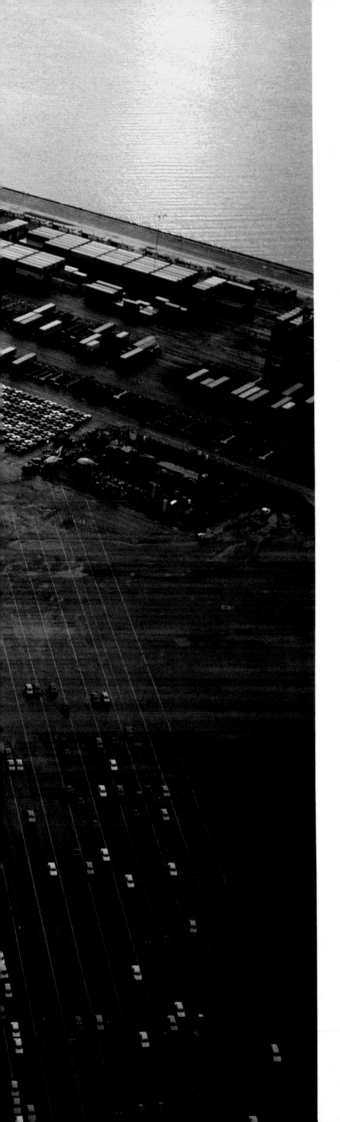

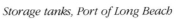

Storage tanks, Port of Long Beach

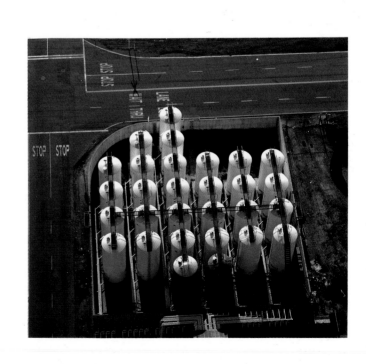

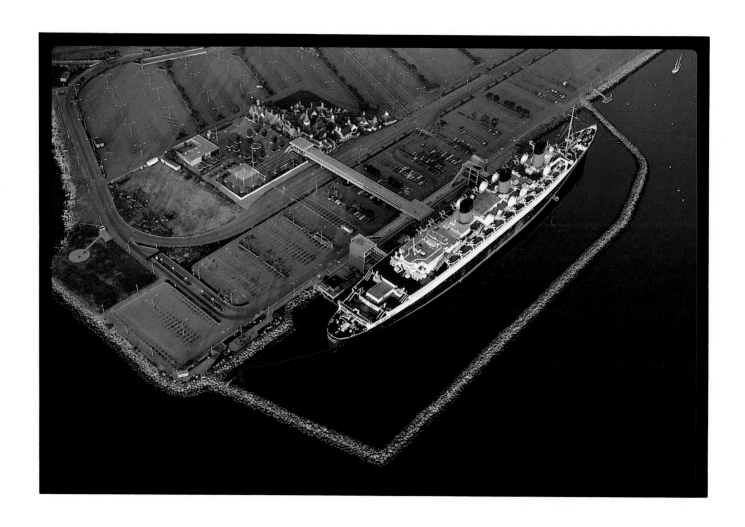

Queen Mary, Long Beach Harbor

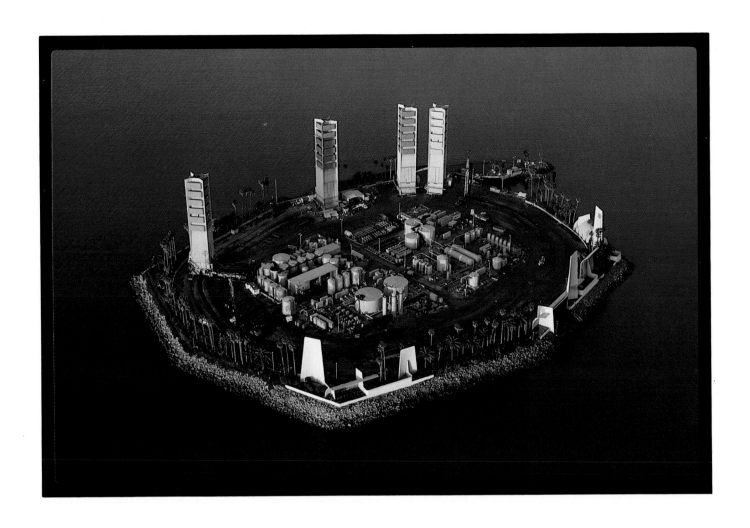

Camouflaged oil island at Long Beach

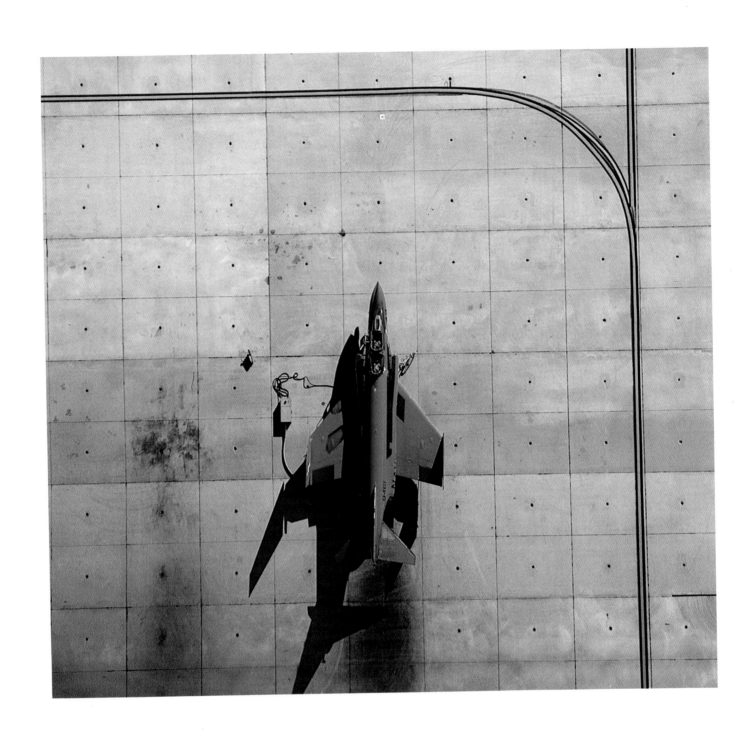

Target drone on the ramp, Naval Air Station, Point Mugu in Ventura County

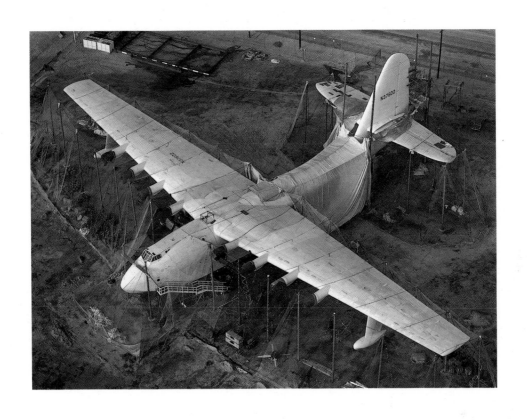

*The "Spruce Goose" of Howard Hughes being readied for
tourists near the Queen Mary in Long Beach harbor*

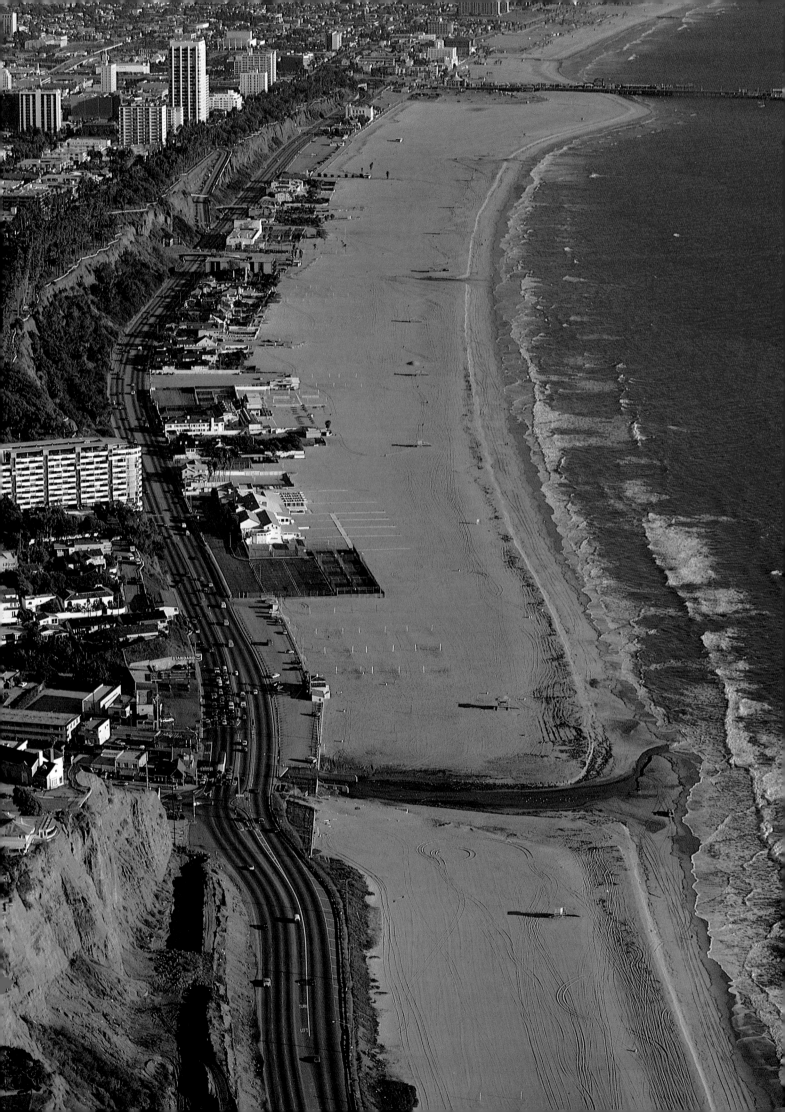

SANTA MONICA BEACH

Jon Carroll

When the Los Angeles smog gets too bad, or the hot wind from the desert blows too long and too hard, you have to head for the beach. When you get there, you're probably in Santa Monica — a small, coastal event fictionalized by Raymond Chandler as "Bay City," with a fictional population made up mainly of brutal cops and corrupt politicians. In real life, Santa Monica is a much nicer place. Turn right and head up the Coast Highway a mile or so, and you're in Santa Monica Canyon, an even smaller coastal event with a large literary history. Bertolt Brecht lived here during his wartime exile from Germany. William Faulkner lived here. Jon Carroll, a writer and editor of national reknown, lives here now. Until recently, Carroll only got to see the Canyon during breaks from his job as editor of New West Magazine. *Then he decided he might enjoy life more as a freelance writer, and he moved into his small Canyon bungalow on a more-or-less full-time basis.*

"The tour starts here," he says, opening a cabinet just inside the front door. "This is an important place that you'll find in every house near the beach — the small corner near the front door which contains The Bag. In The Bag are suntan lotion, playing cards, a bottle opener, spare cash for the guy who comes around to sell you stuff on the beach . . . You see the two beach chairs and the frisbees? It's ready and waiting, so you can leave the house in the morning from now until October."

We start out through a concrete tunnel running under the Coast Highway, leading to the beach. Carroll points out pertinent graffitti.

"LOCALS ONLY, NO KOOKS OR VALS. 'Vals' is short for 'Valleys,' residents of the San Fernando Valley, who are hated enemies in the continuing territorial wars on the beach, which are fought entirely bloodlessly, and by adolescents, and which go entirely unseen (except for these graffitti) by everybody else. The wars are fought by social pressure. Sitting down next to other people, and glaring, and playing radios and yelling epithets.

"Here's my favorite. A LOVE FOR THE OCEAN AND ITS WAVES — THAT'S WHAT SURFING IS ALL ABOUT. And here. CRYSTAL TUBES PEELING OFF INTO THE SUNSET . . . 'Tubes' being exactly what you think they are — that class of wave most desired by surfers. Here's an interesting one. 18 LOSERS. The number refers to lifeguard station 18. Each lifeguard station has its own adherents, who hate the adherents of all the other lifeguard stations."

Reaching the sand, Carroll pulls off his worn running shoes and drops them carelessly next to a low, concrete wall. "It's a Southern California ritual of long standing," he notes. "No one ever takes them." We set off down the beach, south, toward the long Santa Monica pier, splashing barefoot through a shallow, fast-running stream that cuts across the sand to reach the sea.

"This is Will Rogers State Beach, and the interesting part is that there are social stratifications. This area, which has the end of the Santa Monica Channel River flowing into the ocean, is called The Lagoon. It's used by children and their families. The other side of the river is a heterosexual singles beach, which groups around the volleyball courts. Just beyond that, another 100 yards down the beach, is the gay beach, which has no lines of demarcation but is absolutely rigidly defined nonetheless. I don't know how they know. I mean, I know how the latecomers know, but I don't know how the first guy here knows. Beyond the gay beach begin the exclusive beach clubs, which give out their own beach chairs and their own umbrellas and their own towels, all in the same royal blue, or red, or white. That first house there was Marion Davies' beach house for a long time, willed to her by W. R. Hearst.

"The lifeguard stations are rather plush. Gone are the days of that little stool with the ladder up to it. Now they've got slanted, tinted windows, there's a phone inside, and many lifeguards bring radios and televisions. But usually, on heavy days, they're standing out there by the water waiting for drownings. There are about 10 rescues a day on every half-mile stretch of beach on busy days. Lifeguards are low-paid civil servants with not much of a retirement plan and not very good hours, and the ever-present threat of danger for which firemen and policemen get paid a lot, and for which lifeguards don't get paid much at all. The great advantage, aside from all-over tans, is that the girls still cluster around, and they always look good.

"Down there, as you can clearly see, is the Santa Monica Pier, which is one of the last old amusement piers. It has a merry-go-round, bumper cars, all those arcade things where you throw baseballs at milk bottles, and a small boat ride concession. Periodically the City of Santa Monica decides it wants to turn it into something more commercially viable, like fancy restaurants, and in every case the wonderful citizens of Santa Monica have refused to let this happen. That and

Santa Monica, city and beach

rent control are the two big issues in Santa Monica.

"Two years ago we had the Great Flood of '79. There was a huge rainstorm, which meant high seas, and the Channel overflowed and came up to the bottom of the bridge and went 50 miles an hour. Most of us worked all night helping the people who were on the wrong side of the river, and directing traffic — because this is one of the favorite routes into Pacific Palisades, and there was no way to get into Pacific Palisades. I stopped one man and told him there was no way in, and he said, 'But I'm a doctor,' and I said, 'It's not like there's a special way to get in for doctors, *nobody* can get to Pacific Palisades.' One macho guy tried to brave it anyway. He gunned it, and went into the puddle about seven feet and sank right down, and climbed out and stood on his car.

"I saw a dead body on the beach one time. There was obviously nothing I could do for it, so I just ran on, and when I came back they were loading it mournfully into the back of a little yellow pickup truck. I saw several beached seals, and one beached whale, and a wide variety of styrofoam artifacts of all sorts, their colors virtually untarnished, although they may have been in the sea for years. Clorox bottles seem to be a big favorite for some reason.

"On the Fourth of July, Will Rogers Beach is just wall-to-wall people, and the streets are enormous traffic jams. When I first got here, during the summer of '78, people would come by hawking ice cream, half-and-half bars, drumsticks, soda and, occasionally — and entirely illegally — beer. Last year they started hawking pineapple and coconut slices on a stick for a buck, and Perrier. There are also an enormous number of low-flying biplanes carrying banners, moving slowly up the coast line, advertising rock concerts, jeans shops and tanning lotion. Above them are the high-tech skywriting planes, which are actually five planes in formation spitting out smoke which turns into letters, and always spells out 'Coppertone.' I think they have a corner on the planes.

"I discovered another name for Mexicans — the one used by lifeguards. That name is: 'People who don't swim very well.' I heard one lifeguard say, 'I hate to draw Tower Number 6, there's always a lot of people who don't swim very well down there.' Down by the Pier, close to the freeway with plenty of parking, is where people from East LA — Mexicans and Blacks — congregate, and it gets whiter as it gets norther, so by the time you get to the public beaches in Malibu it's all white.

"The most beautiful time of day at the beach is sunset, but the number of people on the beach at sunset is comparatively small. But when it becomes your backyard, you begin to appreciate it in all of its various seasons and moods. I've run on the beach when the fog was so thick and close to the ground that you did not see other runners coming until they were 10 feet away. This being the world center of semi-recreational running.

"Another absolutely ubiquitous sight in the late afternoon are the guys with the metal detectors — big discs on the end of sticks — running them along the sand wearing little earphones, looking for watches, jewelry, change. Somebody told me he found a perfectly good portable radio buried in the sand. They're beachcombers with technology attached to them.

"I'm not sure why high-rise condos haven't taken over the Canyon. It may have something to do with the Coastal Commission. But also I think that people who live in this little pocket have, in general, lived here a long time, and have no interest in destroying it. It's so easy to be content around here that, in some weird way, greed is reduced. You don't sell out to the first developer who comes in waving money, because what could you buy that would make you any happier than you already are?" □

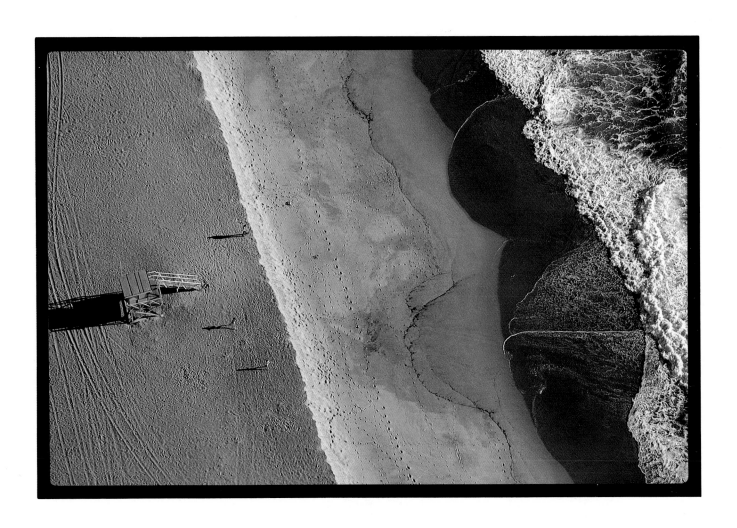

Joggers on the Will Rogers State Beach near Santa Monica

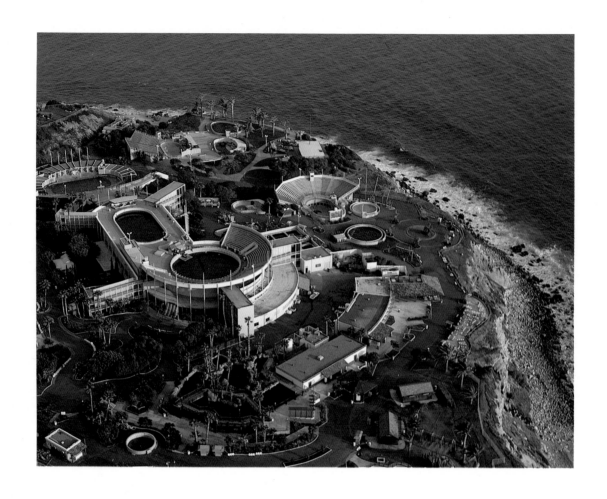

Marineland on the Palos Verdes Peninsula

Right: The last remains of the Dominator *at Palos Verdes Point*

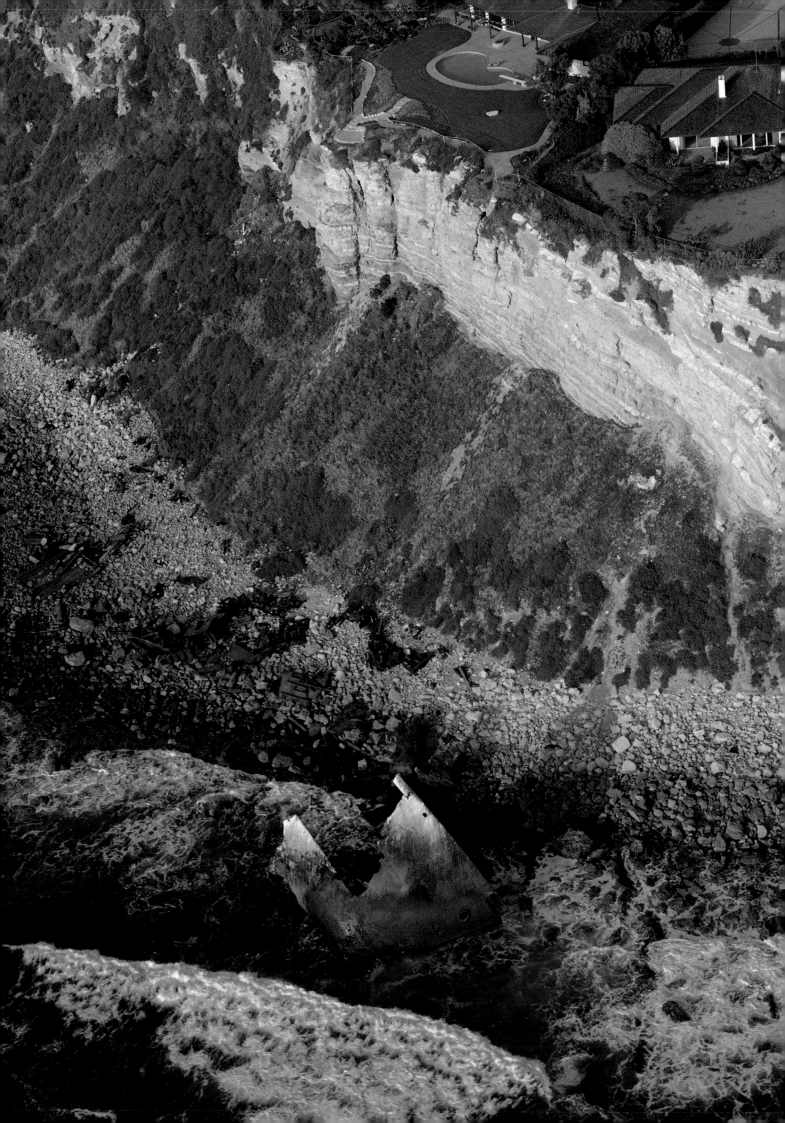

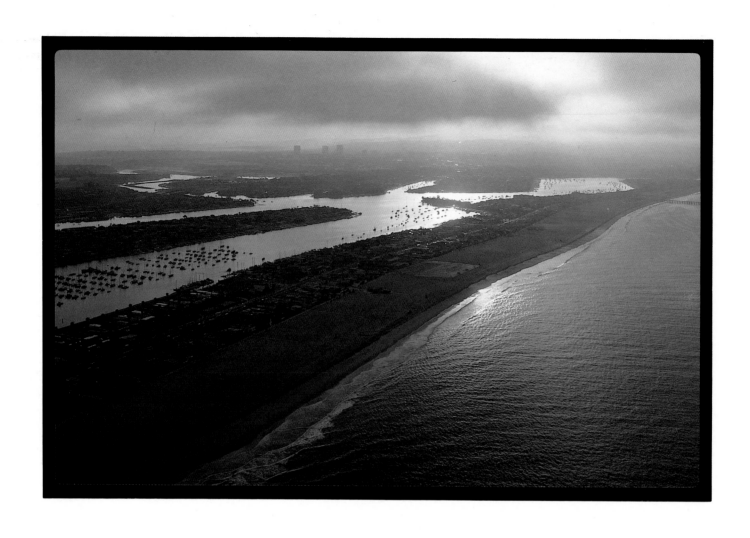

Newport Beach and Newport Bay in the morning

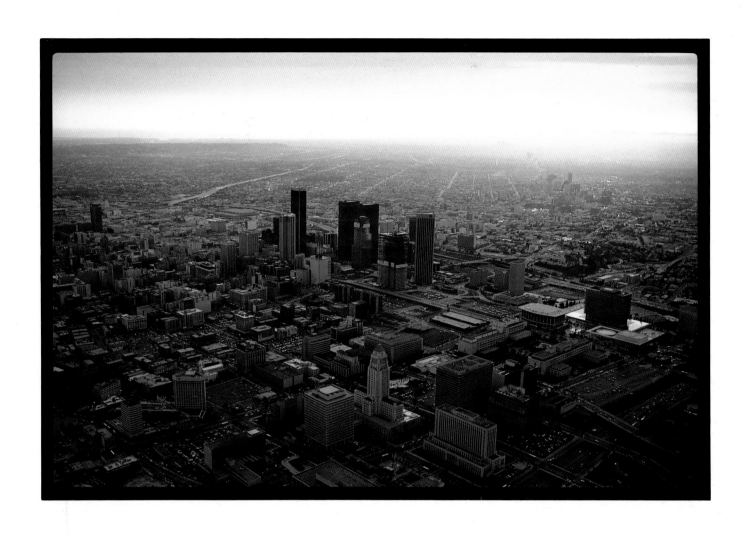

Los Angeles in the afternoon, just before a rainshower, looking west toward Santa Monica

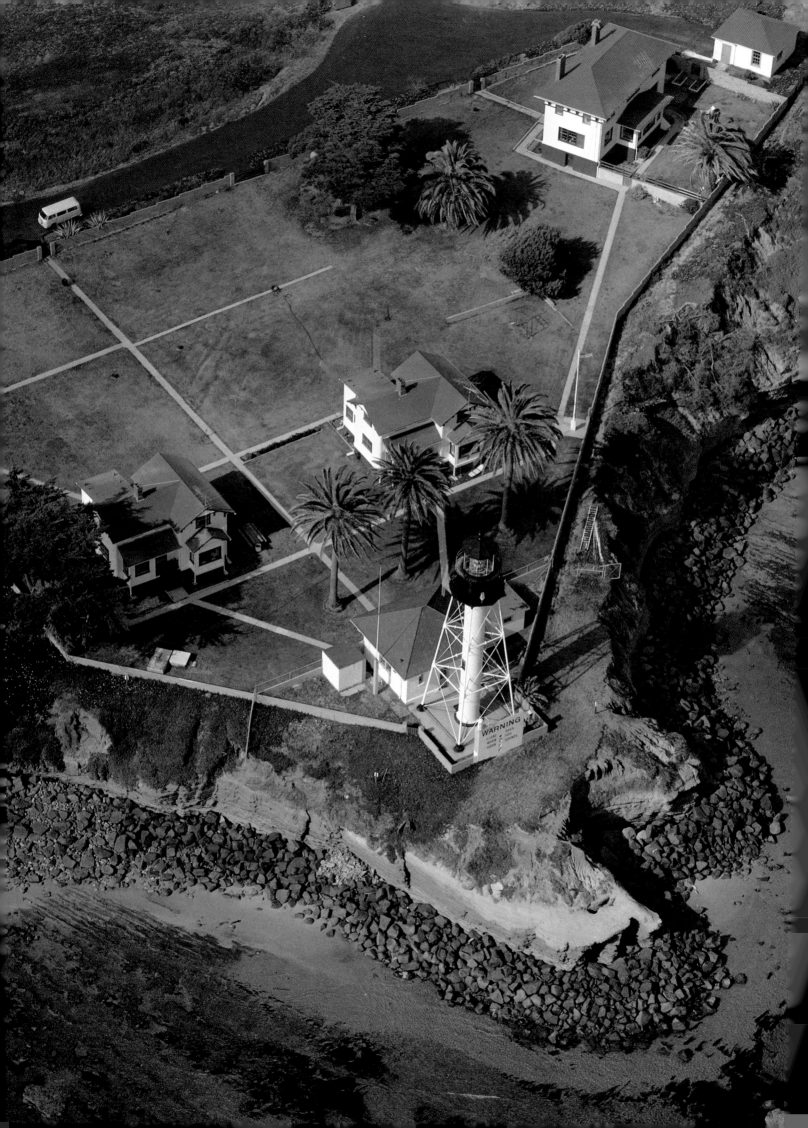

CWO — US COAST GUARD

Terry "O" Gallaher

The Bodega Bay Coast Guard station is built on a spit extending well out into the bay. It has two large state-of-the-art rescue boats. The place suggests a well-run but relaxed police station. Its operating area extends from Point Reyes to the Sonoma-Mendocino county line and out 20 miles offshore. Chief Warrant Officer Terry "O" Gallaher, a matter-of-fact sort, commands 22 enlisted personnel, male and female. They address him as "Skipper."

In comparison to, say, the south Florida waters or even Southern California waters, the Northern California coast is subject to pretty strong storms — coming down out of the Gulf of Alaska — and pretty constant northwesterly winds. Small craft advisories are in effect almost continually because of winds averaging around 25 to 30 knots, much heavier sea conditions, large swell conditions, et cetera. The coast itself is quite rocky, doesn't have the nice sandy beaches that you might run into in Southern California. The water's cold because we have the California Current running along the West Coast here that's coming down from Alaska; the temperature of the water averages around 50-55 degrees. So you're much more subject to hypothermia. If you were to fall over the side in the Gulf of Mexico, your life expectancy would be 24 hours-plus, presuming you could stay afloat. Here in coastal waters, for an unprotected individual going over the side, it might be an hour survival time. It's not particularly for the Sunday sailor.

I've been here at the station for two and a half years and we've had several dangerous rescues. The primary one that I recall was the fishing vessel *Camellia*, about a 35-foot-long steel-hulled fishing vessel operating out of San Francisco that was coming into Bodega Bay in early February of 1979. It was in company with another fishing vessel coming in to Bodega Bay at night, and neither vessel was familiar with the harbor, particularly the *Camellia*. As it approached the outer bay it became disoriented and lost sight of the other vessel and it made a turn that it shouldn't have, and ran right into the Bodega Rock — the large cluster of rocks partially submerged in the outer bay. The sea conditions at the time were quite heavy with approximately 12- to 15-foot breakers rolling in onto the rock. The vessel was able to get a distress call out, a "Mayday" call, and we immediately responded with our motor surf boat, arriving within minutes of the initial call. But when the vessel hit the rock — there was actually a line of submerged rocks to the seaward side of the nonsubmerged rock — and when it came in, a large wave

lifted the boat up and over the submerged rocks and set it down between the submerged rocks and the other rock so that it was abeam to the sea.

As it lay in the trough of the waves, the waves were breaking over it, and it sank immediately. But it was in such shallow water that it couldn't sink any real distance so the stern of the boat was under water and the forward part of the boat was still out of the water. And there were five crewmen aboard. Our boat arrived at the scene immediately, but couldn't get to the boat because of its position, so we called San Francisco and requested assistance from helicopters — standard procedure on a case of this type — and we recalled additional personnel.

Helicopters arrived from San Francisco and illuminated the area with searchlights. The wind was blowing at about 40-45 miles an hour. It was absolutely the worst sea conditions to try and effect a rescue of somebody off a boat. We tried various ways of getting the people off the boat. One attempt was made to use the helicopter to carry a line over and drop it onto the boat; and we got the line over there and the people didn't quite seem to know what to do with it. We yelled to them to try and tell them what to do and they didn't seem to understand. Finally one man was washed off the boat. The others were kind of in the cabin of the boat with the waves breaking over them and we couldn't get them off with the helicopter because the boat was banging around so much. As it tilted from side to side, the rigging on the boat was whipping around so much that it could have possibly knocked the helicopter out of the air if it tried to effect the rescue.

Well, they were still trying to do it using a helicopter basket to try and lift the people out. When we were able to get the one individual who was washed over the side onto the rock, we discovered that four of the five people on boat the boat did not speak English. They were all Korean fishermen from San Francisco. Then a second man was washed over; the helicopter was above him, watching what was going on, and in desperation they lowered their basket into the water and when they lifted up, they discovered that they had caught the man's arm in the basket. He was unconscious. So using the basket they dragged him over to the rock.

A sheriff's helicopter brought the first man ashore, and was going to land to take the second man ashore, when a bird hit the tail rotor and they had to make an emergency landing on the rock. About this time a third individual was washed over the side into an area of high breakers, and one of my boats, a little 13 footer, went in the breakers and was able to pull this man out of the water. He subsequently died from drowning; in fact, two others died also. We ended up saving two of the five people on board. From the time we got the first call to where the last person was pretty well accounted for was around five hours. For that action, two individuals received the Coast Guard Medal, a very distinguished medal, for endangering their own lives, and the station itself was awarded a citation for the whole operation.

Our number one responsibility is search and rescue. That's a traditional job of the Coast Guard dating back to our heritage from the Lifeboat Service. The Coast Guard is a combination of the Revenue Cutter Service and the Lifeboat Service, with one additional function, the Lighthouse Service. The Revenue Cutter Service and Lifeboat Service were joined in 1913 and the Lighthouse Service joined the Service in 1939, and it then became the US Coast Guard. The function of search and rescue goes back to nearly our beginnings in 1789. And that is the number one function of this station, search and rescue.

Our second most important function is law enforcement. This consists of enforcing all laws and treaties in the United States on the high seas. The one that most people would be familiar with with the Coast Guard is our boating safety program where we will board a commercial or pleasure craft, do an inspection of the safety equipment on board, make sure that they have sufficient life jackets for the people on board, the right type of life jackets, check the condition of the life jackets and fire extinguishers and flame arrestors on the gasoline engines and various other pieces of required safety equipment. Most small boaters have probably come in contact with the Coast Guard at one time or another on the boating safety aspect.

A traditional function that's becoming more important today is the interdiction of smuggling. That was the original function of the Coast Guard when it formed in 1789 as the Revenue Cutter Service — for us to interdict smuggling. It was formed under the Treasury Department by Alexander Hamilton, and the whole reason for it was that tariffs and taxes collected on imported goods was the only source of income for the United States. There was such a great deal of smuggling right after the end of War of Independence the Revenue Cutter Service was formed to try to insure that the taxes were collected and went into the national coffers. This has continued until today. During Prohibition the Coast Guard was very active in trying to prevent the illegal importation of liquor. There was a number of actual battles waged between rum runners and the Coast Guard. Today the emphasis has shifted to illegal drugs. Primarily marijuana, cocaine, heroin, et cetera; and this has kind of heated up in the last several years to become one of our major law enforcement functions. There's more drugs coming in, definitely more than compared to, say, 20 years ago. Our culture is shifting to a certain extent to the use of drugs, more common use of it.

The Coast Guard is also responsible for prevention of pollution. We're very much environmentally connected with the coast and we are the watchdogs, really, of the coast, the coastlines and the waterways of the country, and I think it naturally follows our other traditional duties of rescue, life-saving and so forth, guiding commerce. In fact, we're so connected with commerce that as a national agency we're under the Department of Transportation, not the Department of Defense. □

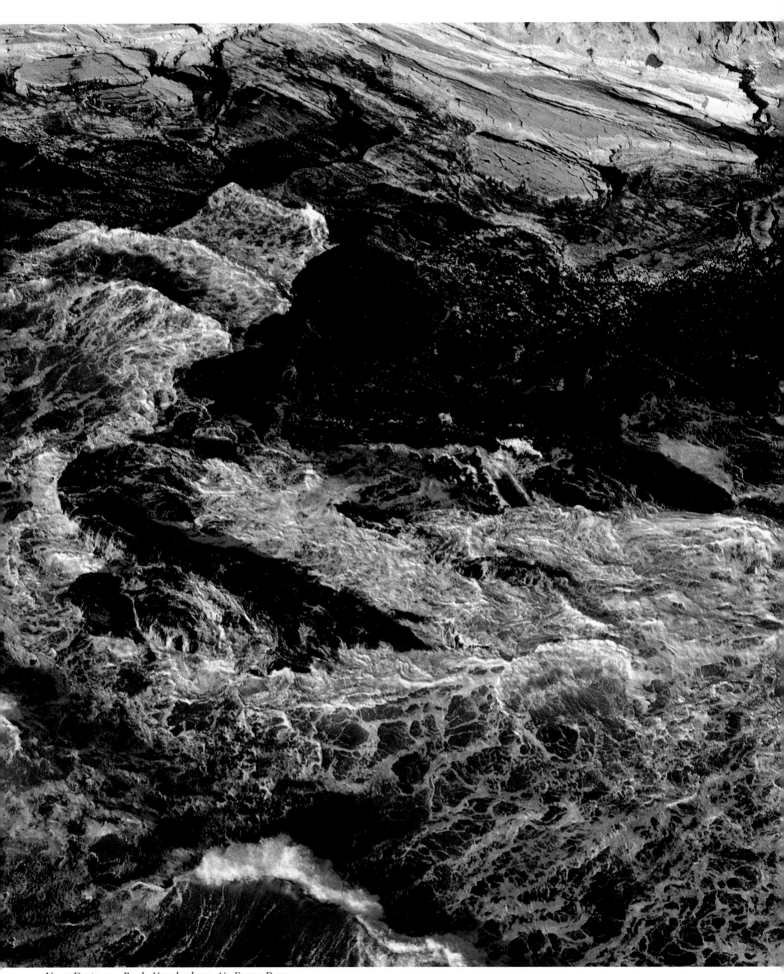

Near Destroyer Rock, Vandenberg Air Force Base

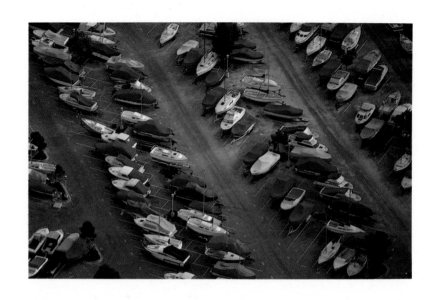

Above and right: Dana Point Harbor, Orange County

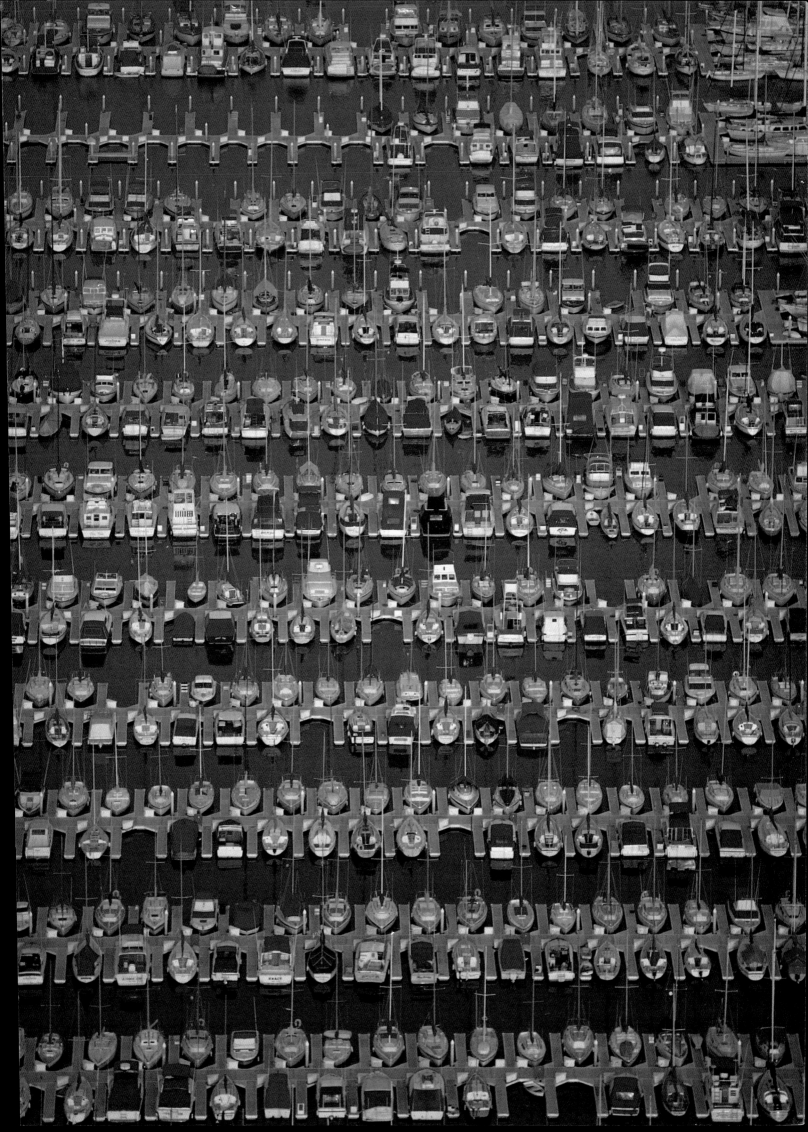

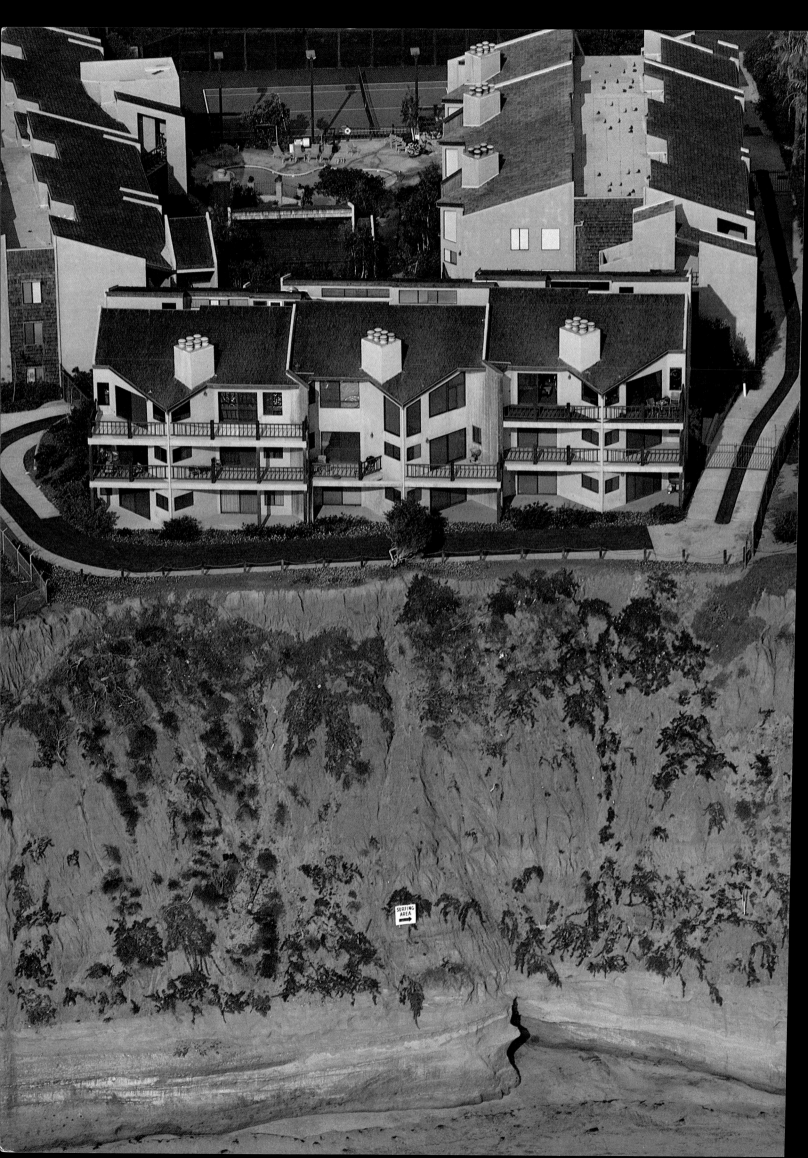

SURFER-OCEANOGRAPHER

George Domurat

George Domurat was probably one of those kids who inadvertently drove adults nuts with his questions. Good questions, mind you, but certain to show his elders their shortcomings. Questions like, "Where do waves come from?" and, "How come the sand dunes look different this summer?" Domurat eventually sought out his own answers. Although he began his college studies as a biology major — "I don't know why; I hated biology" — he soon found geology and geological-oceanography. Eventually he completed a master's degree in oceanography and landed a job with the US Army Corps of Engineering's Navigation and Coastal Planning division in San Francisco. Domurat is a fortunate man. He has managed to combine his surfing avocation with his oceanographic vocation.

My first memory of the ocean is when I was young and swimming at the beach in New Jersey with my mother and a wave hit us. We both started tumbling and all of a sudden I tried getting up and I couldn't because the wave had so much energy, so much power, that it would just pick people up and completely turn you around. You didn't know where you were going. Lots of times I've been very close to drowning because of heavy waves and heavy seas, and those times always scare me. Many times I just prayed to be able to hold my breath just a few more seconds.

I'm 29 now, but still in the ocean. I've been surfing 15 years, so I was always interested in waves. I spent all my summers on the New Jersey shore. There's a very broad, shallow continental shelf offshore there, which reduces the wave energy as the waves approach the coast. Also, the storms tend to move from west to east, so on the East Coast the winds haven't had a chance to build the waves before they hit the beach. On the Pacific Coast, the shelf is narrower and much steeper. And the winds have such a long reach of open space to blow across they have a good chance to build waves.

I first came out here to take this job with the Corps of Engineers. When I got here I went down to Ocean Beach in San Francisco and just watched the waves come in. I was here two months before my equipment arrived from the East Coast and I just watched Ocean Beach and the surfers there. It looked great, fabulous. Finally I went out there with a few other guys and it was just too big. The waves looked about six feet, but when I got

out there they were two times bigger than I was and had much more energy than I was used to. The waves just picked me up like a toothpick and started throwing me around. I was so scared I just prayed I could get out.

Even now, that beach is very, very intimidating. The waves are big and they have a lot of energy. It took me a long time to get used to it. A friend of mine was recalling, the other day, a time when he was riding a wave and it hit him on top of the head with so much force it pushed his feet through the board, snapping it in three pieces. When he got on the beach and took a look at the board — he fitted the pieces together — there were these big depressions where the board snapped. The wave just drove him feet first right through the board.

I surf almost every day. Usually I'll go out in the late afternoon if the waves are good. On weekends, I'll leave at 6:00 in the morning and be back by 9:00 or 10:00. A lot of the guys surfing around San Francisco now are from Southern California. And they're all older. That was a refreshing point of surfing here versus the East Coast. A lot of the East Coast surfers are younger. The old-timers just can't stand 30-degree water anymore.

When I was young, I had the deepest respect for the older kids. They'd beat up on you if you didn't. Now you just don't see that respect in younger kids. A lot of the LA surfers are younger and they're aggressive. That's just the nature of America today; it's a violent place. That's why I like surfing early in the day. I go out by myself for two hours or with just a few close friends. There's a lot of places between San Francisco and Santa Cruz where nobody surfs. A lot of beaches nobody even knows, so you can always find a place to yourself.

I didn't come here just to surf. The job with the Corps brought me here. I have a master's degree, but I was up against three PhDs for the job. They picked me because of my experience with the ocean — my (scuba) diving and surfing experience. Being in the water, knowing what the waves are like and actually feeling them — not just knowing the mathematical theories — is important. As an oceanographer, you ought to be able to go out in the field, look at the conditions and describe what's going on. When somebody's house is falling in the water and they're trying to figure out why, you have to be a soils geologist to analyze the sands, and also look at the beaches, the waves. You gotta be able to explain, on the spot, what's happening.

Basically, there are three types of waves: waves generated by the wind; waves generated by seismic activity of the earth — earthquakes and undersea landslides; and gravitational waves formed by the attraction

Along the beach in San Diego County

between the earth, sun and moon.

The wind waves are a function of the pressure on the sea's surface and the frictional drag between the wind and the surface of the water. You get a little wind blowing on the surface and a ripple starts to form, just like blowing over a bowl of soup. Once this wave gets formed you have a steep side to this water field, and the wind can continue blowing against that steep face and the wave gets bigger and bigger. But it reaches a limit called the "steepness factor." Roughly speaking, that's a ratio of one to seven: a one-foot wave will be about seven feet in length. "Length" is the distance between the top, or peak, of one wave to the next peak. Once it gets beyond that limit, we get a breaking wave.

Seismic activity can cause "seismic sea waves," or *tsunamis*. These waves are very, very long — on the order of a thousand miles in length. So, if you're out in the middle of the ocean, such as during the Alaskan earthquake, you might get a half foot deflection in the surface of the ocean. You wouldn't even know the wave passed by. As it approaches land mass, however, it starts to concentrate, creating the monster waves you see in disaster movies.

There's a lot of misconception about tidal waves. The tide is actually a wave and it travels around the earth. It's formed, essentially, by the earth's mass, which is rotating, and the gravitational attraction of the moon and the sun trying to pull the water away from the surface of the earth.

Waves can be classified in terms of wave length, which is related to period — the time it takes for one crest to pass until the next comes. You start with a ripple, then move into a condition we call a "wind wave" or "the sea." These will have periods here in California of two to ten seconds. Then we have a "swell," with periods of ten to twenty-two-plus seconds. These are generated by large storms far offshore — a couple thousand nautical miles or more. Then you get into a "surf beat" or "wave groups," where some of these waves get into phase with each other and form a packet of waves. Finally, you have the seismic waves and tidal waves, where the periods are upwards of twenty-four hours.

The predominant wave direction in California is from the northwest. During the spring and summer, however, when the southern hemisphere has its winter, waves have been monitored coming from the South Pacific and reaching Alaska. This is called the "southern swell." If you look at a globe, you can trace a great circle route from the Indian Ocean to California, and waves can come that far.

The Corps of Engineers has 35 wave gauge sites spotted up and down the coast. One type, a "pressure gauge," monitors the change in pressure as the wave form passes over the top, so it gives us the amplitude, or the height of the wave, and its frequency. The greater the pressure, the greater the height of the wave. Another type gauge — named "wave rider" — is a buoy about a meter in diameter that floats on the surface. It has an accelerometer inside so it senses the acceler-

ation which the buoy experiences as it rises up and down. That gives us the height and frequency of the waves. An underwater cable from the buoys carries the information to shore. There, the data is sent through a phone line to a computer in San Diego where it's automatically analyzed and we get the statistics out. Within two minutes after the data is sensed in the ocean, we have already analyzed it.

Our computer communicates directly with the National Weather Service. We send this data to them and they give us three-hour updates on the marine band weather radio, which is used by recreational boaters, fishermen, search and rescue operations, shipping companies and surfers. The primary use of the information, though, is by the Corps of Engineers for dredging operations and beach erosion projects — studies as to how, why and where erosion occurs.

There really isn't erosion, it's just a dynamic process that's occurring. The ocean takes care of itself, and you can see it in everyday processes like dunes. Sand dunes are a natural storage area. As wind and big waves start eroding the beach, the beach is moved offshore to an area where the waves don't have quite the energy and they start breaking up. That's where the sand starts sinking and builds a bar. The bar starts forming, making that area shallow. So instead of the waves breaking right on the beach, the waves are now breaking on the offshore bar.

The building of the bar varies with the season. During the winter, you'll see waves breaking way offshore because that's where the bar is. That's nature's defense of the beach against storms; the wave energy is partially absorbed by the bar rather than on the beach. And when the storms slacken in the spring and summer, you start to get beach building as the material is scrapped off the bar and slowly moved back up to the beachheads.

The dunes are formed by wind. You go to any beach that has some dunes and, at low tide, you'll see sand moving. Layers of sand just moving across the face of the dunes. If an obstruction is placed in the way — a stick or a log — you'll start seeing sand collecting around the stick. Well, that's essentially how dunes are formed. Then you'll get some seeds and something growing around the stick and then grass.

I have total respect for the ocean. I let the ocean do what it wants to do. I have one picture of a 60-ton boulder that was moved by waves. The boulder was bigger than a four-wheel drive truck. The power of the sea is just awesome.

I find the coast a place to relieve stress, a place for me to relax. I sit out there and wait for the waves and reflect on things I've done and will do in the future. It also can be a very bad place to be. I work with the ocean and never try to work against it. I'm just a visitor. I also have the deepest respect for the organisms in the ocean. Man doesn't belong there; it's the sharks' water, and when they come, I leave. Something drives me to study the sea and be around it, but I have no fights with it. I could never win. □

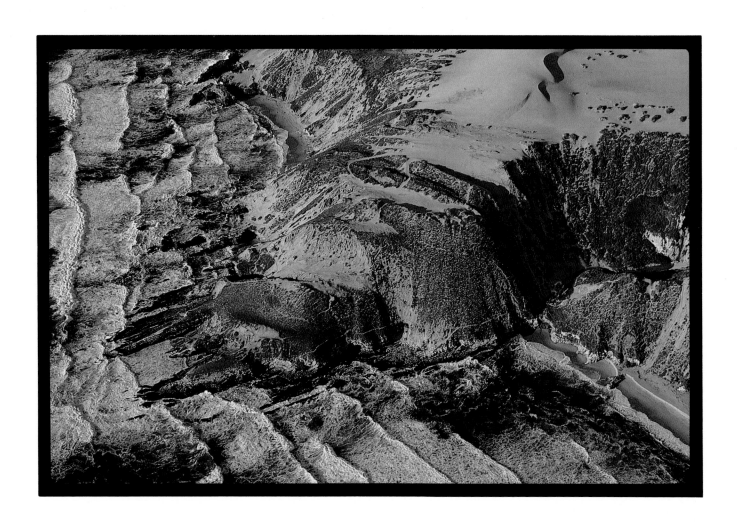

Point Sal, just north of Vandenberg Air Force Base

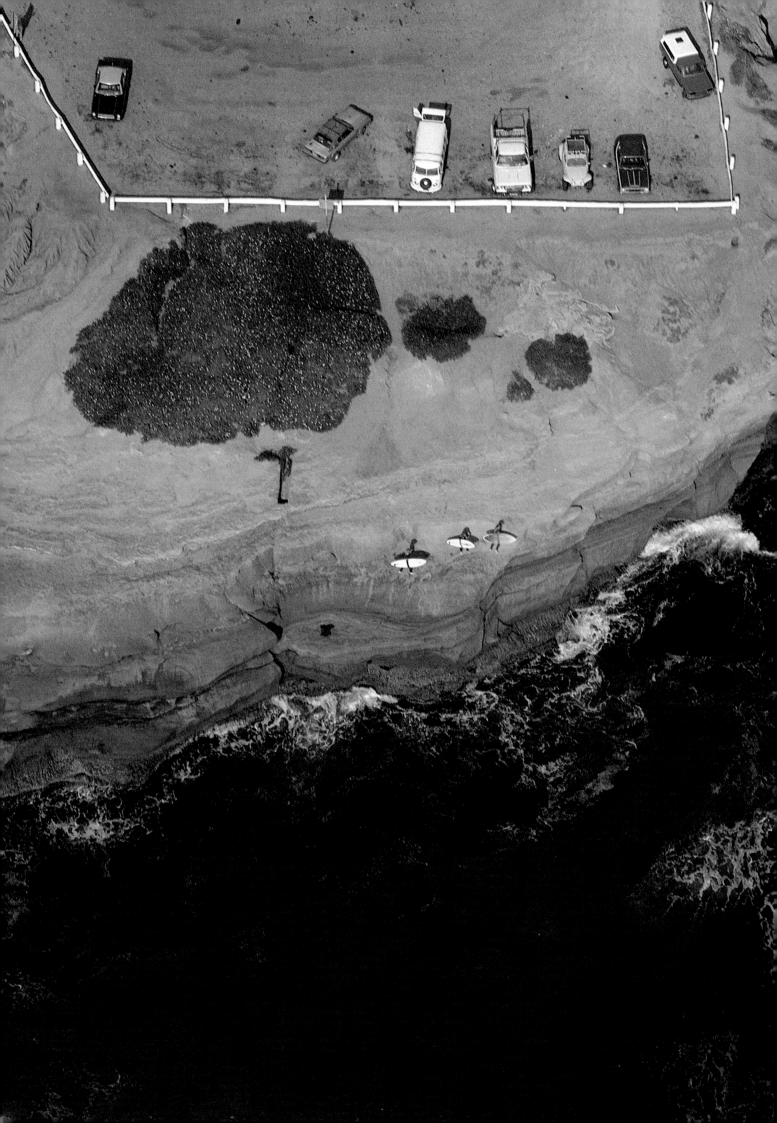

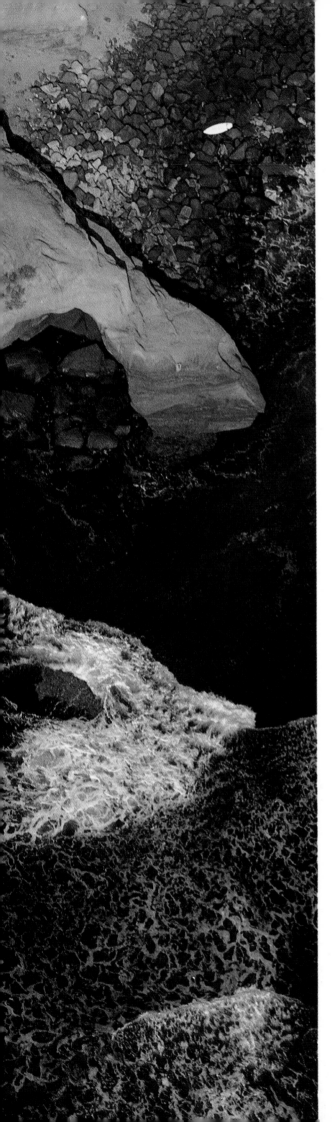

Surf & Turf Travel Trailer Park near Del Mar, San Diego County

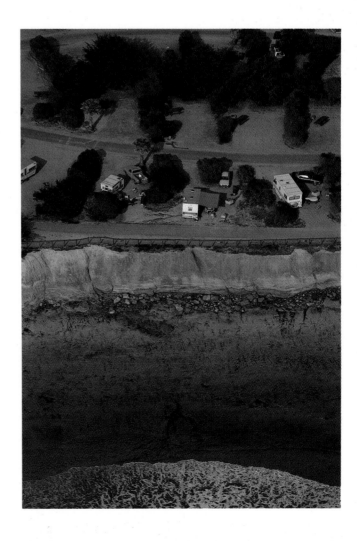

Surf & Turf Travel Trailer Park near Del Mar, San Diego County

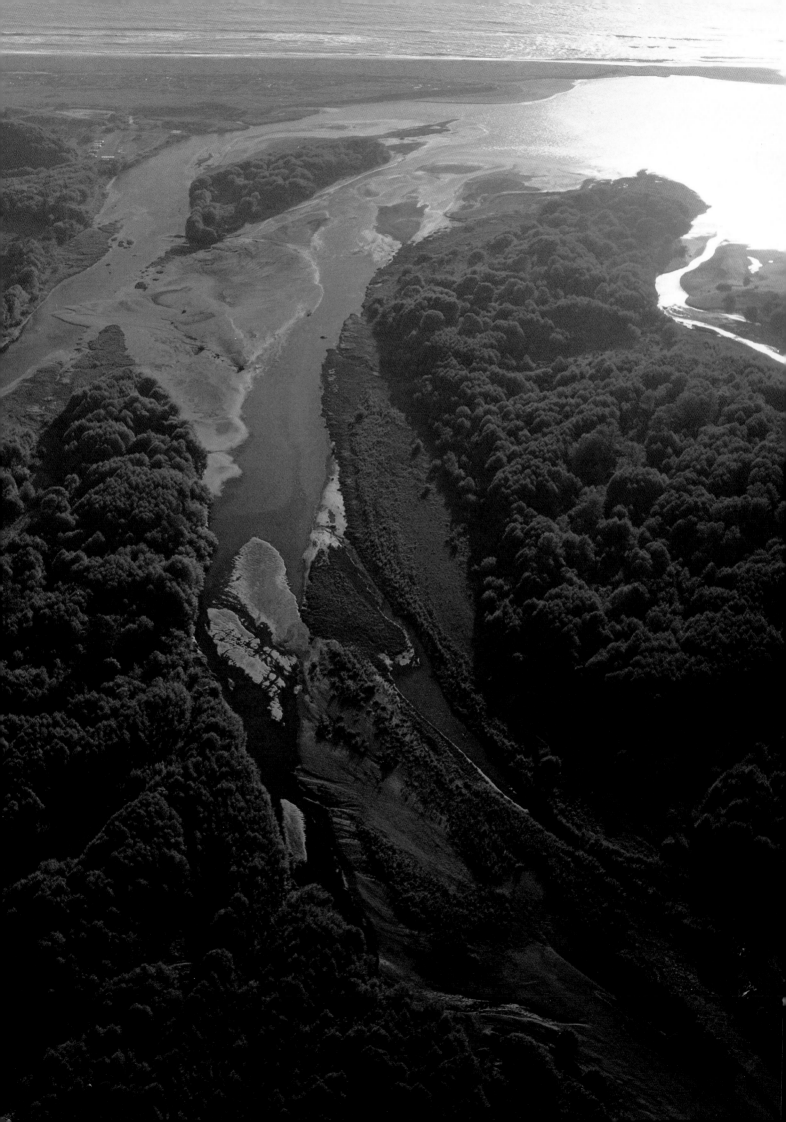

TRIBAL SPIRITUAL LEADER

Loren Bommelyn

Until the mid-19th century, Indians lived comfortably along the Pacific Coast in villages and even towns with hundreds of dwellings. Like today's coastal inhabitants, many lived in houses hewn of redwood. It was a lifestyle basically unchanged for tens of centuries; California north coast Indian artifacts have been carbon-dated to 3500 BC. The area around Crescent City, some 20 miles from the Oregon border, was Tolowa tribe territory. The Tolowa numbered perhaps 2000 when, in 1853, the settlers of Crescent City were responsible for the first in a series of massacres aiming for total extermination of the tribe. By 1900, only 110 Tolowa remained. A spiritual leader of the Tolowa, Loren Bommelyn, a young teacher, has made an extensive study of his people's history and way of life. He teaches Indian language and culture at two north coast high schools. Bommelyn believes he is the only teacher in the US credentialed to teach Indian language and culture. When he speaks of the old culture, he draws upon scholarly research probing back into ancient times, and also upon recollections of the older members of the present-day Tolowa tribe, suggesting a continuity of civilization extending from before the days of Tutankhamun's reign in Egypt.

They were a sea-going people. In a book written by Steven Powers in 1872, he writes of the Smith River Indians having had a boat that was 32 feet long, 8 feet-four inches wide; it was highly polished, a thing of beauty. It sat lightly and evenly on the sea. It was a huge canoe, capable of carrying 25 men. They had long, slender paddles, and they'd line up men on both sides, standing up, and they'd stroke the water. No sails at all.

And they utilized the land, too. They had a vast resource of food. Salmon came in schools — they flooded the river, huge herds of salmon. And there were elk and deer herds numbering in the hundreds. They used to burn the mountains in certain areas and keep it grassy so the elk and the deer would stay there. So they could just go up there and kill elk or deer when they needed to. They say that on Lake Earl, when the fowl would fly in on the Pacific flyway, they would darken the sky for minutes. There's all the crustaceans and clams, and seafish like perch, and surf fish like halibut and red snapper and black snapper — just a vast amount of food. And off the rocks they'd get murre eggs and eagle eggs. They'd hunt sea lions; harpoon and eat them.

They had a code: The sea was to be highly respected. You never point at the ocean. To point at it was to insult it. You don't point at people, you don't point at the sea. You're supposed to nod your head toward the ocean. Because the ocean is a vast mystery — it was powerful, it contained things we'll never totally understand, things we'll never see, that are still unknown. It was very highly respected. You didn't needlessly play in the ocean water, the waves; you went there to catch fish and that was all. You didn't challenge it like that. They called it the "big river" — it could take your life like *that*.

The Indians here were very permanent residents. Contrary to the nomadic life on the plains where they lived in teepees that were easy to take down, on the coast they lived in plank houses. Plank made from split wood. They would bring down the redwood and then they would split it. They'd make a canoe out of part of it, and they'd make their houses and other stuff out of the other part of it. Their houses had four walls, about 20 by 25 feet; a plank structure with planks anywhere from two to four inches thick and, say, a foot to three feet wide. They would dig a pit one to three feet deep and line the floor with flatboards, and build a fireplace in the middle. They'd have a pitched roof with a ridge running across the top. No chimney; they'd lift one of the long boards on the roof, depending on which direction the wind was blowing, and it would suck the smoke out.

The rich men, their houses had maids and servants and henchmen, and their daughters would be sold for a high price. Everything had value. There was a barter system and there was money. If I wanted to trade food for food or goods for goods, that was one thing. But if I wanted to purchase a canoe or maybe get married, I had to use what they called "ventalia," a white mollusk shell, very hard to find, which was their form of currency. It was traded from the Pacific Northwest to California. They would scrimshaw designs on the shells to make them fancy, decorate them with a certain type of snakeskin.

All summer long the people would work. They would catch salmon and they would kill deer and they'd dry it and smoke it, and they'd gather acorn and all the fruits and they'd dry and store it for winter. All summer long they'd work like chipmunks, and then when fall came it was time for celebration. And they'd celebrate from fall all through winter until spring again, and then they'd go back to work.

Men wouldn't need a lot to wear in summer, maybe a loincloth. Women just wore a hula skirt, nothing on top. In winter they had coats made of hide or of fiber, and a pointed reindeerskin hat. Some men might wear elk hide. When they dressed up to dance, that's when they

Mouth of the Klamath River at Requa, Del Norte County

put on their really ornate dresses and aprons, a lot of beads and basket-style hats. Real high work, real nice design. It was time to show off, a great occasion.

Art was a way of life. If somebody made a particular kind of regalia, that was an art. People were known for their basketry. Maybe somebody was good at tanning hides. Maybe there was a good drum maker. People got names for what they were good at. Everything you made was artistic; everything you made or produced had your personality in it. It was all incorporated as one thing, all together.

Their days started before daybreak with a bath in the ocean or river. Everybody, even the children from the time they were born. My aunt said everybody got up in the morning and went down to the river *every* day — dead of winter, too; not just summer. There would be frost on the ground and your lip would be shaking, and you'd take a bath. The men slept in the sweat house, and they would just go out and dive in. The sweat house was a sauna type of thing. To bathe, they used a dried wild lilac, blue; they call it soap flower. It grows on the coast.

That's the way the day started. By the time the sun went down, they were in the house, definitely. The only people that walked around at night were called "det-nany," meaning night-walkers, evil people, practitioners of sorcery. They would try to use black magic to kill people. So good doctors would have to undo their work. Everybody prayed, but doctors did prayers for a long time.

In the morning they prayed toward the east. Anthropologists interpreted this to say they were sun-worshippers, but this wasn't true. They faced east because that was the new day coming. They prayed to the almighty god. There's one god. At the end of the day, they looked toward the west, toward the water. Heaven existed across the water, on the other side of the shore; when you die, you cross the water and you go to heaven. I asked the old people if they talked about hell. The Yuroc tribe has a word for hell, but to the Tolowa tribe, hell would mean eternal death. Because when you died, you went to a better place, better than here. An eternal happiness. That's where they got the nickname of the happy hunting grounds, I guess. Dying and going nowhere, eternal death — that would be hell.

They looked at the world as all things having a purpose. On a spiritual level, they were in tune with things. Like today, America is physically oriented; a lot of people relate to things in terms of physical responses. But they were spiritually oriented. They had spiritual friends and allegiances that told them things. Our Bible was the universe, and we studied the animals and the plants and the water and the seasons to find our path in life. That was our Bible a long time ago. □

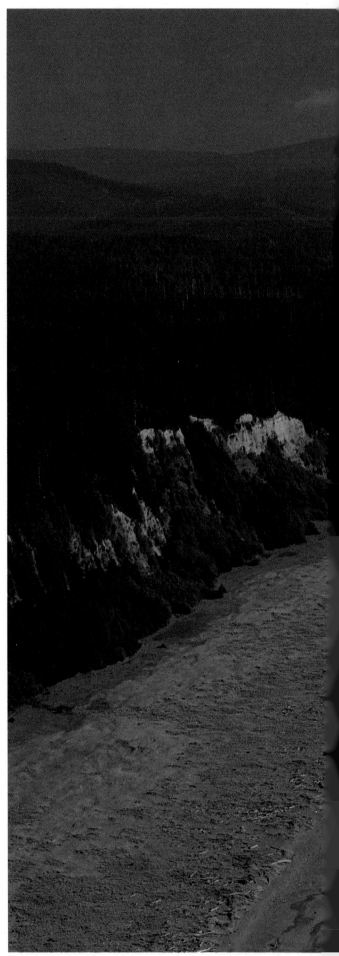

Prairie Creek Redwoods State Park in Humboldt County

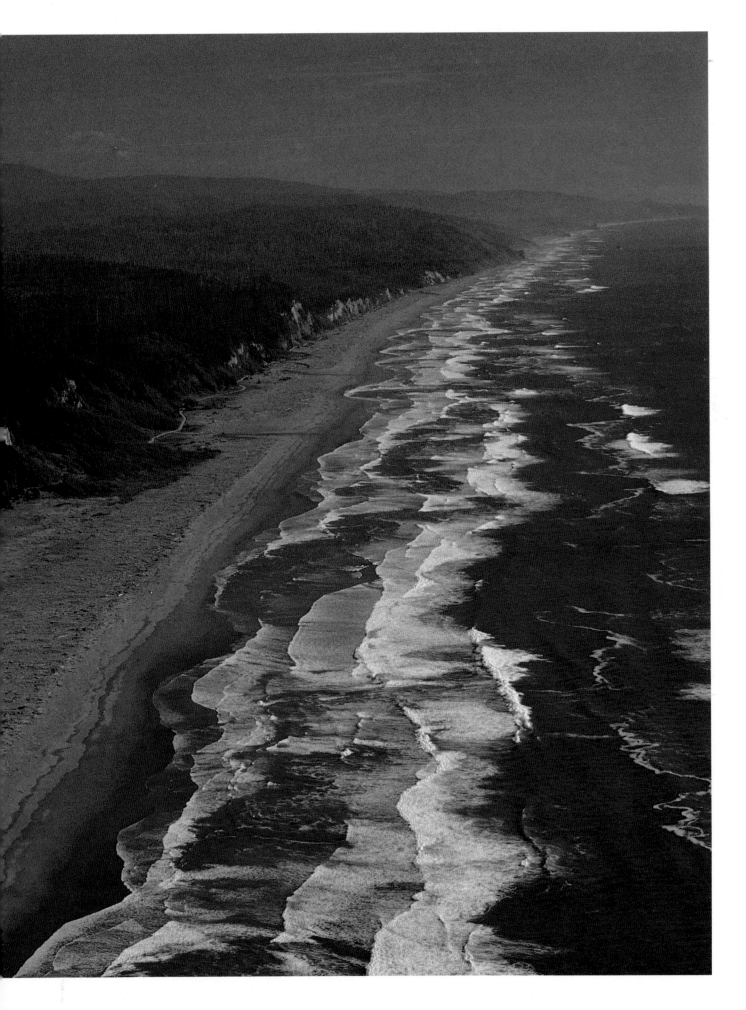

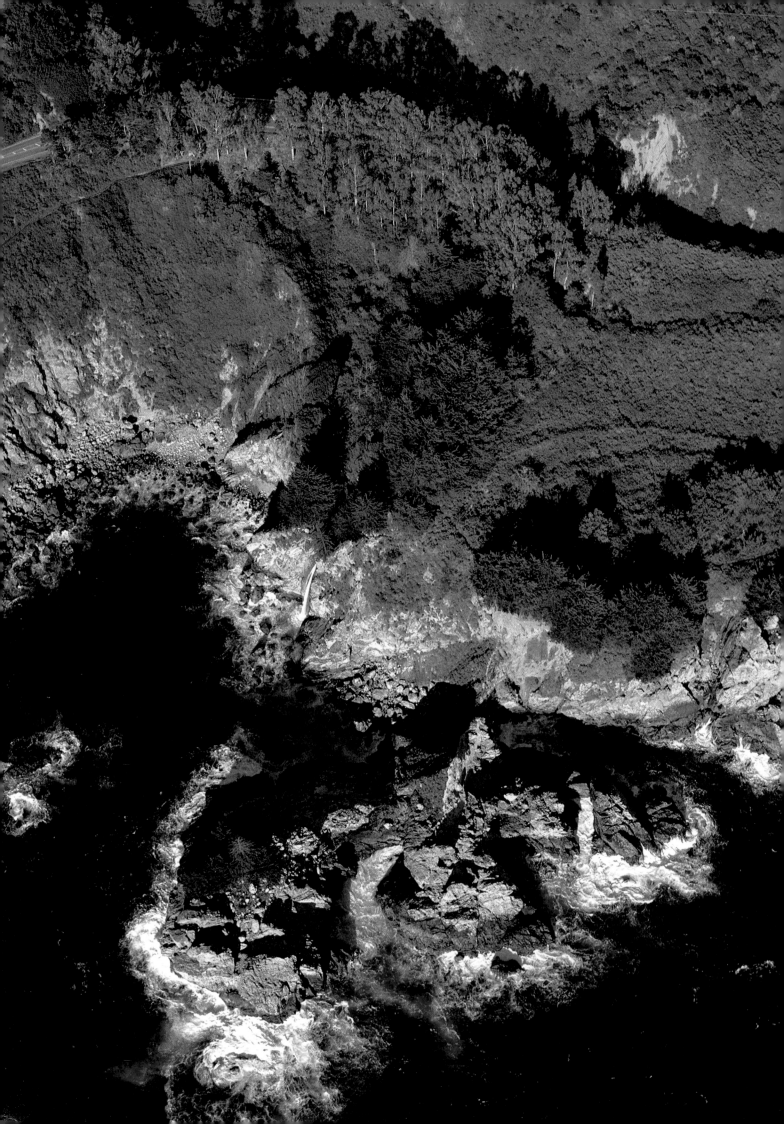

E S A L E N

Michael Murphy

Once upon a time, just a couple of decades ago, there was no human potential movement. There did exist, however, a broken down spa on a breathtakingly precipitous slant of California coastline roughly midway between San Francisco and Los Angeles, and a pair of young academics who thought that this might be an appropriate place for people to come and explore ideas and experiences with a kind of relaxation and depth impossible to achieve in most academic settings. One of these young men was Michael Murphy, whose family owned the old resort, and who had, indeed, grown up on the Big Sur coast. One thing led to another, and soon enough, Esalen sprang forth. At the start, Arnold Toynbee and Aldous Huxley taught there. Later, as Esalen became less academic in nature, more experience-oriented, came Fritz Perls, the father of gestalt therapy, and Ida Rolf, who spread the gospel of her radical massage therapy, known today as "rolfing." In no time, Esalen became the fabled international epicenter of Far Out, and springboard for the human potential movement. From his Mill Valley home, Murphy recalls with great fondness the gathering of forces that was to become Esalen.

We wanted a forum to explore different ideas, and we wanted to combine Eastern and Western perspectives on the human condition, on psychology, science and religion. Here was this piece of property that we thought was perfect for having retreat-type meetings. As time went on, our interest and the interests of others who came into the program shifted the emphasis of the programming away from merely talking to ex-periencing, through things like meditation and other awareness disciplines.

The setting down there worked beautifully for that. First there is the separation. It's about an hour from Monterey, which is the closest town. There's no radio or television at Esalen: you can't get television, and radio reception is poor. The mailman comes once a day and brings in one or two newspapers, but there are 150 people living in that community so the newspaper never really circulates. People are isolated there and that reinforces the mood and the intensity of the experience. This leads to a particular vitality and people talk about it as a power spot and make up rather fanciful terms about it.

But you don't have to get occult to explain this. It's the power of that land and the isolation.

Another thing that contributes to the intensity is the fact that you are pushed so strongly against the ocean and the mountains. Where we are it goes up to 2,000 feet at sharper than a 45-degree angle; it's one of the steepest coastlines in the world. We're perched there on that ledge, and you get the sense that there's no retreat. You have to face into this infinity, both the Pacific and the high mountains. Gerald Heard — a philosopher who was one of Aldous Huxley's mentors — said the sharply rising mountains behind us had a psychological effect on everybody on that ledge. The ledge is about a mile long and it varies in width from 50 to 200 yards. It's that perch on the edge of the Pacific which suggests the fact that you might not be able to retreat from these infinities that are of the sea and the sky and the land behind you.

The contrast of the elements contributes to the emotional charge often found in our programs. For example, you can have a brilliant sunny day and then a storm will come rolling in, and you have a vivid contrast happening within half an hour, and you'll see rainbows across the sky, and you'll have brilliant shafts of sunlight cutting down through the clouds, then you have this wide sheet going from blue to blue-green to gray. Tremendous contrasts. I've imagined that the place has the kind of contrast that Ireland does; the mysticism of Ireland resembles the mysticism of Big Sur in that respect. The sharp contrasts of mood that come from the sharp changes in the weather have also contributed to the power of the different moods or spells that come over that property during these workshops.

We didn't design any of this. It just grew out of the interests of the founders, Richard Price and I, and the other people who came in. It worked synchronistically with what we were doing to intensify mood and, at times, insight: the isolation of the place, being perched on a ledge at the foot of these high 2,000 foot mountains facing out into the Pacific and up into the heavens, and the sharp transitions in weather. When my grand-father bought the place, he believed that there were only a few places where you got the combinations of waters — salt water, fresh water and hot mineral waters — coming together in such abundance, and so he had bought it way back in 1910. He was a doctor and wanted to build a spa in the European tradition.

And you have the combination of elements: there's a canyon on the property that goes in about three miles. You can move from a very harsh, bright sunny day into this dark redwood canyon full of ferns. We once had a geologist down there who claimed there were over 20 micro-climates on that property in this mile of coast. He took me around and showed me how you can

---

Near Julia Pfeiffer Burns State Park, Monterey County

move from a hot, hard atmosphere to a very cool, moist one in 200 yards. Big Sur as a whole is like that; people are attracted to it because of the range of mood that is generated.

What were your backgrounds?

Dick Price and I both had graduated from Stanford University in psychology. He had done graduate work at Harvard in psychology. I had done graduate work at Stanford in philosophy. But as an undergraduate I had become interested in Eastern philosophy and particularly the work of Sri Aurobindo, an Indian philosopher who combined an evolutionary perspective on the world with Indian transcendentalism. That combination attracted me and it's been a primary influence on my thinking ever since. After graduate work at Stanford, I went to the Aurobindo ashram in India, and spent a year and a half there studying meditation and Indian philosophy. I started Esalen with Dick in 1961. Dick's background was similar to mine. He got interested in Eastern thought and felt dissatisfied with academia and liked the idea of starting a center that would delve into subjects that the universities weren't interested in in those days; the psychology and philosophy departments just weren't dealing with those issues then.

My grandparents had planned to build this big beautiful place on the cliff and my grandfather thought he was going to realize his dream of building a spa, but he couldn't. There was no highway there until 1937, and he went back to practice medicine in the '40s because the other doctors had gone off to war. After the war he was 85 years old and he died in '48. In a strange way, Esalen is a fulfillment of his idea. It's like a spa; people come to take the hot baths. But the emphasis is much more psychological and spiritual. Spas were always supposed to be something like that.

When we moved down there in '61 it was a very different place. It had a wild bohemian beginning. Hunter Thompson was a caretaker my grandmother had hired, just 22 years old. Joan Baez lived there for the first year we were there; she hadn't become famous yet. Henry Miller was taking the baths practically every day and lived right down the road. Emil White, the painter, was Henry's great friend, and still lives at Esalen; then he was our neighbor. In effect we had to establish law and order, because the police force didn't get down that far from Monterey. It was just this old resort. There were less than 1,000 people living on the Big Sur coast, which is 80 miles long.

So here was this facility being run in a kind of crazy way by some people my grandmother had rented it out to, an evangelical church group. At the same time, you had all these other people living there: a young counterculture sitting next to the evangelical fundamentalist church group. Then on weekends the gay crowd would come into the baths and more or less take over on Friday and Saturday night. This was a crazy combination of elements, a clash of forces.

There were some incredible confrontations down there between the factions and one night it ended up — the climactic night. We wanted to find out what kind of arrangement the First Church of God of Prophecy had with the gay crowd that was coming down, because they seemed like unlikely bedfellows. A fence separated the long walk down to the baths from the lodge that was built there. We tried locking it up at night because the place was getting a little scary in the summer of '61; there had been some fights, real blood fights, with no police or anything. But we couldn't lock it up unless we stayed up all night, because soon 40 or 50 guys would appear and steal the locks. We went down to the baths one night and heard this thundering herd. It's all these gay guys who had taken the lock, and they knew we were there. They tried to get us involved in this big fight.

We went out and found Hunter Thompson, Joe Hudson (who was part of the Joan Baez group), and another guy, each of them with a doberman on a leash, all of them had guns — six of us with three dogs against about 40 guys who wanted to take us on. They were mad at us and looking for a fight. These two male dobermans started fighting over this female doberman and the barking was horrendous. We got them apart and started down through the parking lot to kick everybody out, down past the lodge to the baths which are about a quarter of a mile away, and there's no one there. We started back up and the two male dobermans start fighting over this female again and again this barking occurs. About 10 minutes has elapsed during all of this.

We come to the edge and we see all these guys bailing out into their cars and the entire place being evacuated and their cars are all headed south. Instantly we knew that they were afraid we would get the highway barricaded from the north. If we had called up the Monterey County Sheriff's Department and said there was a gang war going on down here, they would have barricaded the highway. So they were all headed south, where there are more side roads to escape.

And that was how we took over. We turned around and there was this couple standing there and I said to them that I hoped they weren't disturbed by the fight; they said, "What fight?" And I said, "All this barking." They said, "We just thought this was a very pleasant looking place and we just drove in." They were our first customers.

We took over in October of '61, but it was not until the fall of '62 that we really got the programs going. It took us a while to get the place organized; our first brochure advertised a series of programs for the fall of 1962, and it started with four seminars. But there were so many people that we had to do six seminars to handle all the people who came. So in the next brochure instead of four seminars we had 13, and they all filled up. The place has always been fully subscribed. The idea was just right.

In the early days of Esalen, did you have any trouble from the forces of law and order who might have thought you were a little too far out?

No, we never did. A lot of people were smoking marijuana and in the early days taking LSD. We set a policy that we as innkeepers had to kick everybody out, "86" them, if they sold anything in the lodge or smoked anything in the lodge. We didn't go into the rooms. I checked with the law enforcement agencies and found that you can't go into a person's room without a search warrant. Our legal duty was to make sure that people were not selling or consuming drugs on the public grounds. There were constant rumors that we were about to be busted either by the FBI or the CIA or the FDA. We always checked it out with our friends in Washington and Sacramento, and they said no. There was a sense at the Sheriff's office that the place had always done all right; there hadn't been any murders.

By about '67 the Big Sur area got to be very wild; between '67-'69 it was really a mecca for the counter-culture and people were coming in from Paris to camp under those bridges. There were always 30 people under the ends of the bridge over Hot Springs Creek, and it's on state property, so we didn't have the legal right to kick anybody out. They had formed these gigantic nests under the ends of these bridges. That reached its peak in '67-'68, the Summer of Love. But then the Big Sur land owners rose up together around 1969 or '70 and evicted all the squatters.

We actually didn't get any publicity until late '67, though we had been thriving since the fall of '62, and in certain ways some of our most creative period was over when the media caught up with us. There was a media blitz about us in '68 and '69: it was nude bathing and encounter groups and that's the image people have of us. What was actually going on was far more complex.

Esalen was widely imitated; there were a lot of centers modeled on us in the late '60s. Most of them have passed away now, although there are 10 or 15 still remaining in the United States and there's a lot of this in Europe and Latin America, and now we even have an exchange going with the Soviet Union.

Why did you decide to leave Esalen?

I moved to San Francisco in '67 to start a center there. My idea was to have an urban center, along with our Big Sur retreat. In those days there was great excitement about the human potential movement, sometimes very naive. And I missed seeing the 49er and Giant games, and liked living in the city. But the main reason was to start that center. I've lived here ever since.

But I go back down about four times a year and spend two months out of twelve down there. For me the intensity of that place makes two months just about right. Dick Price lives there eleven and a half months. You have to have a temperament suited to the Big Sur. Only a small percentage of people can truly make peace with the mountains and live there permanently. For most people it's an intensity to go to for a while. □

Evening along the Big Sur coast

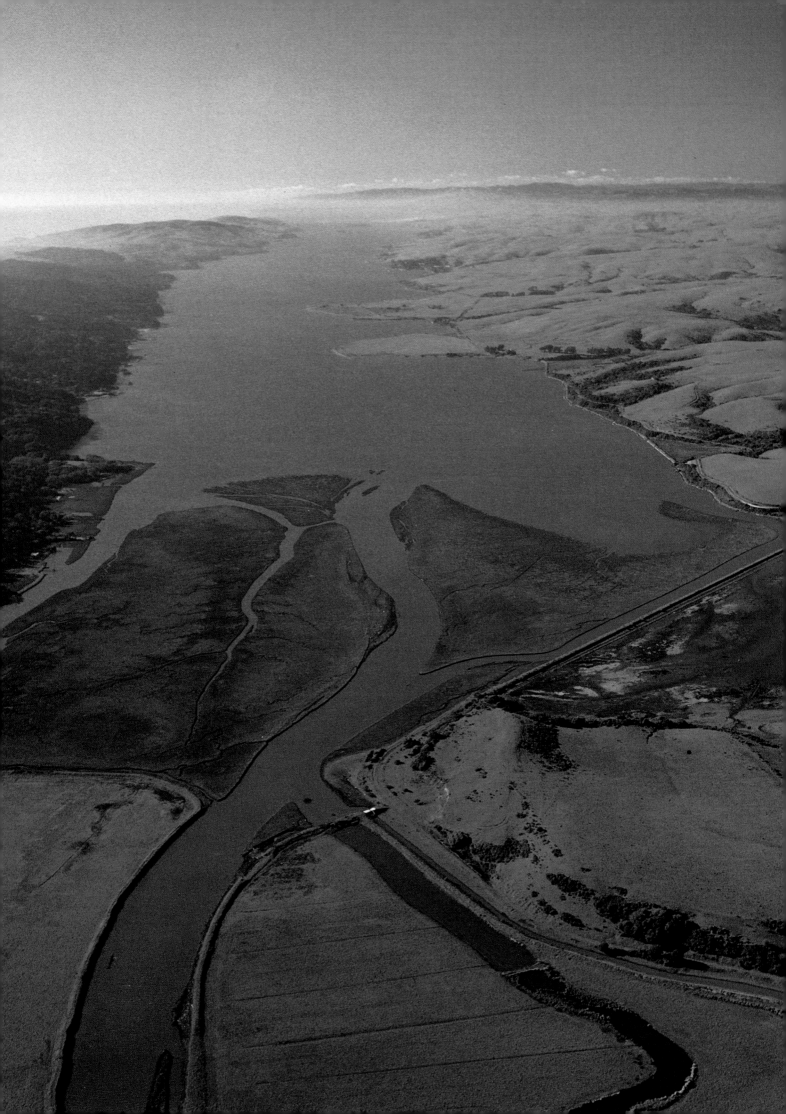

FROM HERE TO ECOTOPIA

Ernest Callenbach

In 1980, Ecotopia — comprising what used to be northern California, Oregon and Washington — seceded from the United States, closed its borders, and set about establishing a survival-oriented, "stable-state" way of living that included ritual war games, collective ownership and operation of farms and factories, strict conservation laws, and an aggressive reforestation program bordering on tree worship. Science fiction? Yes, but Ecotopia, *a charming (and refreshingly optimistic) speculative novel by Ernest "Chick" Callenbach, is a particularly political brand of science fiction, designed (as was Sir Thomas More's* Utopia*) to pose serious theoretical options in clear, concrete, entertaining terms. Callenbach, editor of* Film Quarterly, *a respected cinema journal, and an editor at the University of California Press, published* Ecotopia *himself (with ten friends) in 1975. When Bantam Press noticed how fast his small printing was selling, it brought out its own edition in 1977. Between the two, nearly 200,000 copies of the book are now in print, and Callenbach finds himself a hot item on the college lecture circuit, and something of a reluctant hero to many of the ecologically-oriented. Nor has he been resting.* The Art of Friendship, *co-authored with Christine Leefeldt (Pantheon) came out in 1979; he has just published* The Ecotopian Encyclopedia For the '80s *(And/Or Press); and he's virtually completed a "prequel" to* Ecotopia *variously working-titled* Ecotopia Emerging, Ecotopia Rising, *or possibly (despite jeers from certain humorless types)* From Here to Ecotopia. *Callenbach sat under a shady tree at the edge of a stingy, green lawn surrounding the UC Press office and, over the roar of steady traffic, shared an Ecotopian perspective on the California coast.*

I think of the coast as this very beautiful, fertile, exposed, curved expanse facing out onto the Pacific — which is a very big ocean, the biggest ocean in the world. George Stewart, in his book *Storm*, calls it something like, "space so vast as to defeat Time the Ancient and cause the calendar to lose a day." It's a heavy ocean. The Atlantic is sort of cute and friendly in comparison. I realize it can be dangerous too, but compared to the Pacific the Atlantic is a lake.

And here we are, stretched out in our little, banana-shaped Ecotopia, looking out on this water monster that stretches practically halfway across the world. And that's a very dramatic thing — the border between the land and the ocean here is just a super-dramatic thing.

Now I don't know very much about geology, but I do know a couple of things which add to this drama. One is the San Andreas Fault, running through the coast and out under the Tomales Bay, which is one of the geological boundary cleavage zones in the world's so-called tectonic plates. The shore side of this fault is moving south, the sea side is moving north, and it's one of these stupendously majestic and slow and powerful things that happen on the face of the earth that most of us are not conscious of day by day. But when you stop to think about them it really is an extraordinary process that's going on under our feet.

All these geological processes are very interesting to me because they operate on such a remarkable time scale, and they dwarf human beings. They are so unimaginably vast, and we are so unimaginably petty — even with all our atom bombs and all our technology, we're just twerps on the gigantic breast of mother earth. We are still very puny little critters, and I think it's a good thing for human beings to realize that. It's good for us to keep a sense of proper scale, lest we get carried away with our own razz-ma-tazz. The coast helps you to think about these things.

I have found that when I get into some kind of emotional bad spot in my life, I head for the water. There's something very restorative about getting back to the coast, and there's an interesting biological history aspect to that, because it is widely (although not universally) believed by people who study what you might call the "proto-history" of human beings that our very distant ancestors evolved on the shores of large bodies of water — either the large lakes in East Africa or the ocean, the Indian Ocean along East Africa. One of the reasons being that a coastal environment provides a lot of high protein food that's easy to catch — clams, oysters, shellfish, various kinds of sea creatures like that. There is even an astonishing theory that we went through a period of living as aquatic apes. So we humans, as a species, may be particularly akin to the seacoast. That may be our place.

There are a lot of other things that make people feel good on the coastline, like negative ions in the air. Negative ions are produced in large numbers by water-falls, and by the surf along the sea, and they make human beings feel good. All the things negative ions do is not really known, but they have a pronounced effect on one important body hormone called serotonin. The absence of negative ions makes people kind of crazy. When there's a hot, dry wind from inland — the *santa-ana*

Tomales Bay, Marin County

in southern California, the *foehn* in Germany, the *mistral* in France — people go coo-coo, because the hot wind produces positive ions by blowing over dusty areas. Air conditioning produces these positive ions, too — or rather it takes out the negative ions, which are sort of de-ionized by the metal walls of the air conditioning conduits. One of the reasons people feel so rotten in high-rise, closed circulation buildings may be because the positive ion atmosphere is just not good for human beings. Anyway, people who live by the coast get lots of negative ions.

The coast is not only a boundary between the land and the water, it's where our worst mechanical and industrial actions bear their bitter fruit.

It's a dump, you mean. It's only recently that a lot of people have realized what the ecologists have been saying all along — that everything has to *go* somewhere. But there is no such thing as a true dump, a place where you can really get rid of things. They don't go away. When they were dumping atomic waste out near the Farallones, people believed, I think honestly, that that would make it go away, like flushing something down the toilet. Well, of course it doesn't go away.

So now we realize that the oceans are eco-systems, with their own circulation patterns, and their own life patterns, and people are less willing now to believe that they can simply be treated as garbage dumps. But there are still plans to dump a lot of atomic waste in deeper trenches.

It's basically very encouraging though. I like to find good news where I can, and there *is* good news about the sea otters and the grey whales and the brown pelican. These are three major success stories along the coast. The otters are spreading back along their original range. The grey whales are no longer in danger. And I went out sailing in the Bay here about a year ago, and off Richmond there were a dozen pelicans floating around happy as clowns, and they're coming back in large numbers. As long as you stop doing evil, nature will recommence doing good. It's really amazing, the capacity of the biosphere to regenerate itself once we stop chewing it up.

I'd like to see the redwood forest, or some kind of forest, reestablished in all the coastal areas where there used to be forest. One of the first things the Ecotopians did when they seceded was to put in a gung-ho forestation program. Sacramento has been spending some state money doing this kind of thing lately, which is really terrific, because we can never have enough wood, that's rule one. And we have all this dampish, coolish territory along the coast that used to support immense stands of redwood and other wood. We ought to help that

stuff come back. On a pure money basis wood is one of the highest profit crops you can have, and there are a lot of other reasons why we should have more wood than we do.

Do you have any thoughts about how we can make the coast accessible to people without overwhelming it in the process?

One of the things about the damage-by-people issue is if large parts of the coast are closed off to public access, that puts more pressure on the parts that *are* available. So the general tendency to open up coast access routes in the last ten years is very much to the good. We are, in this, following a tradition of many other enlightened societies in the world. In the West Indies, where they have a terrible tendency for the tourist industry to overwhelm the native population, there are stringent laws about how any West Indian can walk on any beach, and no white hotel owner or New York vacationer can say the nay. That principle is being increasingly extended all over the world, and I think that's a very good thing, because we are a very numerous society and the coast is a very scarce resource. Little by little the ancient property rights along the coast have been modified. There are a lot of legal debates about this, of course, but that's what laws are for, to balance property claims and social interest.

Little by little we will learn better manners in our shared public places. We've made a lot of progress in these respects in the last 10 or 15 years. It's easy to forget that we've actually come a long way. Look at Carmel. Here's a very built-up area where a lot of people live very close to the ocean, and yet the ocean front — which is not a wild ocean front by any means, there are houses all along it within 100 feet of the ocean — is a very beautiful ocean front, and for certain stretches it seems to be perfectly acceptable to have things like that, as long as there's good public access.

There will probably be other places like Sea Ranch where they've been in an intense struggle over whether a land owner should be able to keep other people out or not, and there you'll end up with a sort of quasi-public park. That's the likely pattern for a lot of large private holdings along the coast.

Then there will be outright parks. Oregon is a model for us to follow in this matter. They simply bought up the entire coast, and it's essentially just State Park from one end to the other. I wish we could have been able to do that in California 100 years ago, but we were not as smart as the Oregonians. Still, I think people are really determined to maintain their access to the water — it's almost an instinctual thing. It's a very strong need. □

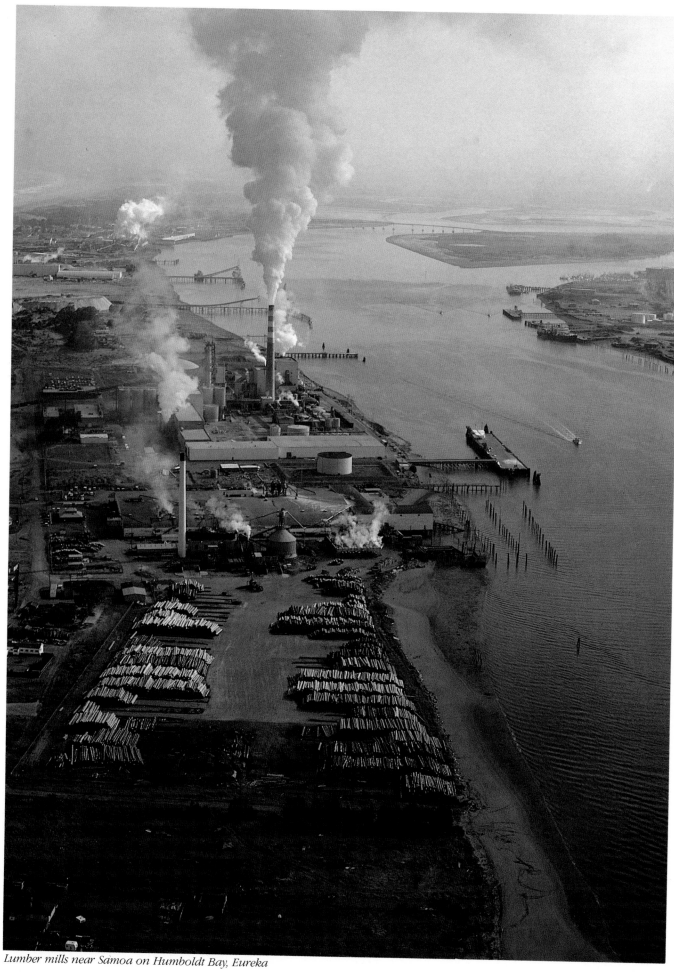

Lumber mills near Samoa on Humboldt Bay, Eureka

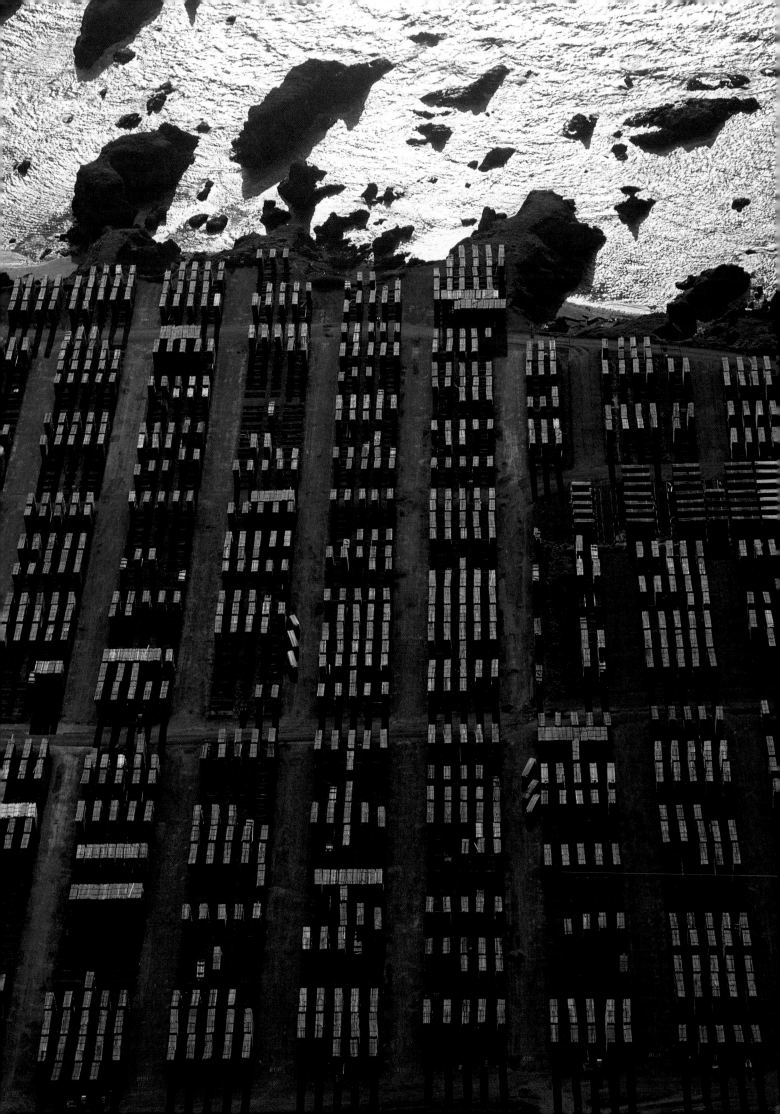

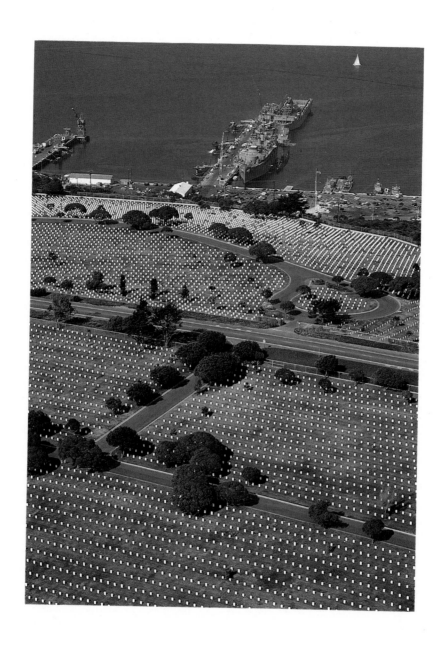

Fort Rosecrans National Cemetery, Point Loma, San Diego

Left: Lumber storage at the mill in Fort Bragg

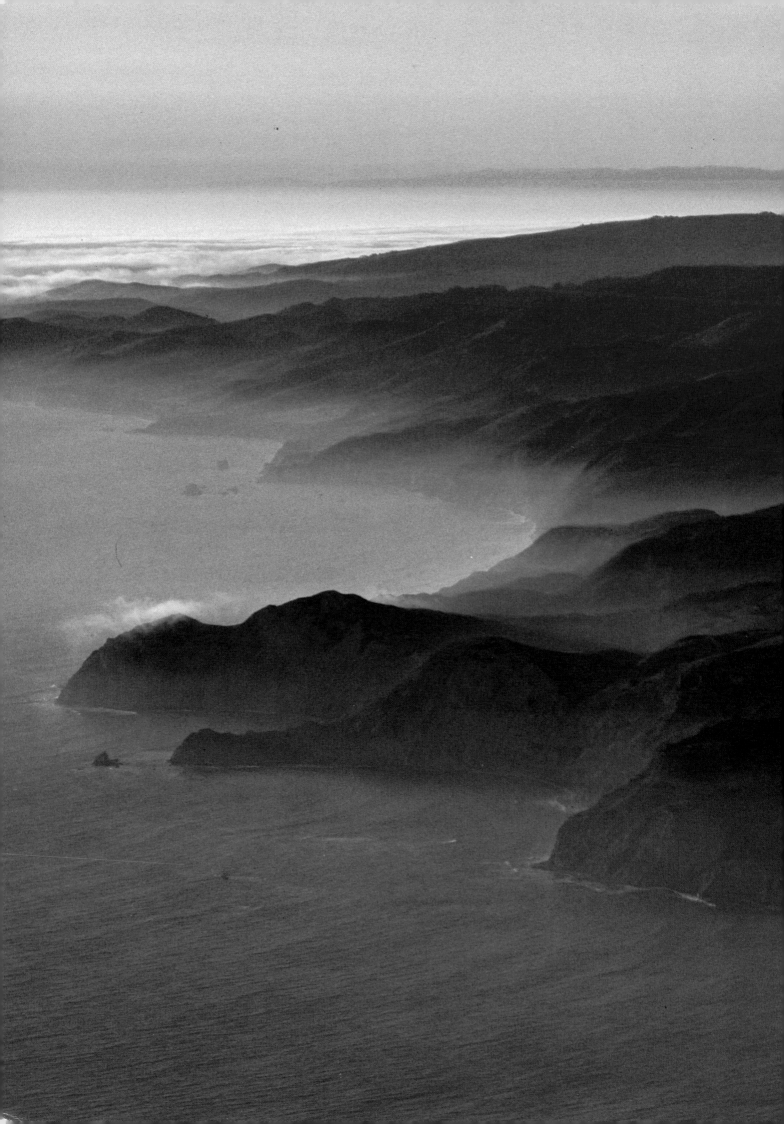

THE NEPTUNE SOCIETY

Richard Jongordon

For many people throughout the United States and the world, California and its coast are symbolic, sometimes literal places for birth and especially renewal. In 1980, for approximately 190,000 people, it was also a place of death. About 30 percent of that number chose not to be buried but cremated. And the ashes of a large portion of that number were scattered at sea. In the mid-'70s, Richard Jongordon brought the Neptune Society to Northern California as a way to facilitate cremation and the scattering of ashes in a dignified, meaningful manner. To be sure, the Society is not a charitable organization or even a non-profit one. But its fees are modest, and for many Californians it provides a graceful link between the living, the dead and the coastal waters. Jongordon describes the procedure.

We usually take several families out on the boat, the *Naiad*, at one time. I'm talking about the immediate family, usually four to six members, sometimes as many as eight. And we usually have three or four families at one service. This is an economy for the family, but it also shares the moment with other families who are having the same experience.

We ask the families to relinquish the privacy of the bow or the stern to each other so each ceremony is separate and private. The family gathers on the bow around the minister or clergyman that it brings along or we provide. The minister says a short prayer and then speaks about the individual very briefly. Then each family member is given a flower to scatter on the sea. Sometimes they bring flowers from their own gardens. Then they step to the rail above the scattered ashes and reflect for a private moment before tossing a flower on the sea.

We then move the boat a little bit to a different position and scatter another set of ashes. When the ceremonies are over, the captain will circle the boat around the flowers on the water. Then, slowly, the boat will back away from the scene, turn and head for home. It's a very nice ceremony that has good feelings and vibes for people because it's in tune with life and in tune with nature and in tune with our feelings at that moment.

Most of the time, of course, the ashes are spread on the sea from the air. The family has a memorial service at their church and asks us to scatter the ashes. But I remember one family that wanted a party on the shore while the ashes were scattered. The plane circled the beach a couple of times, about 500 feet off the water

— real slow circles. On one pass overhead we scattered three dozen roses so they'd be floating down. Then we circled again, scattered the ashes, dipped the wings and flew off. The family had their ceremony and that was it.

Another man died and his wife and children and her brother, who was a Catholic priest, had a little ceremony right on the beach. They said they had spent a lot of time at the shore together and they wanted to know if they could scatter the ashes themselves. I said, "Why don't you just walk out kneedeep like Christ did and scatter the ashes in the water," so they did. Most people don't know you can do that.

People are turning to cremation and the scattering of ashes for two reasons: one is the pull of simplicity and the other is a push away from the old, traditional system. There is the theory that all life emerged from the ocean and when we're through we return to the sea.

So, if a body is placed in a casket and put in the ground, everything, in time, will disintegrate back to the earth. Then one day the rains will come and wash the remains back to sea. What we're offering is the same process, just more directly.

One thing we can't do in California is bury a body at sea. It's not *against* the law, but the law does not provide for it. You might say it's against the law by reverse condemnation. The State of California just will not give a burial permit to bury a body in the ocean. Oregon, however, allows you to do so providing you go beyond the deep (continental) shelf, which is about 30 miles out.

California is a unique, trend-setting area. People here on the coast are more open-minded and they question things more. They're more willing to reevaluate old traditions. There are a lot of younger people who are the naturalist- or Sierra Club-types who believe that nature is very important, and that the ocean is an important part of nature.

Today in California, about 30 percent of the deaths are cremated. But in New Zealand and Australia, it's about 70 percent. England is about 80 percent, Japan is 90 percent, and Sweden is about 95 percent.

We have approximately 50,000 individuals who have joined the society and paid the $20 membership fee. Our families are signing up at about a rate of 1,000 per month and have been for quite some time.

But this type of service absolutely couldn't have started in, say, Omaha. Not necessarily because the ocean isn't there, but because the same mentality isn't there. They're too Baptist, too Bible Belt, and cremation or scattering the ashes is not acceptable. Those people just haven't thought about it enough.

Like I said, the sea is a very important part of the cycle of life. And death. □

Evening fog along the Point Reyes National Seashore, Marin County

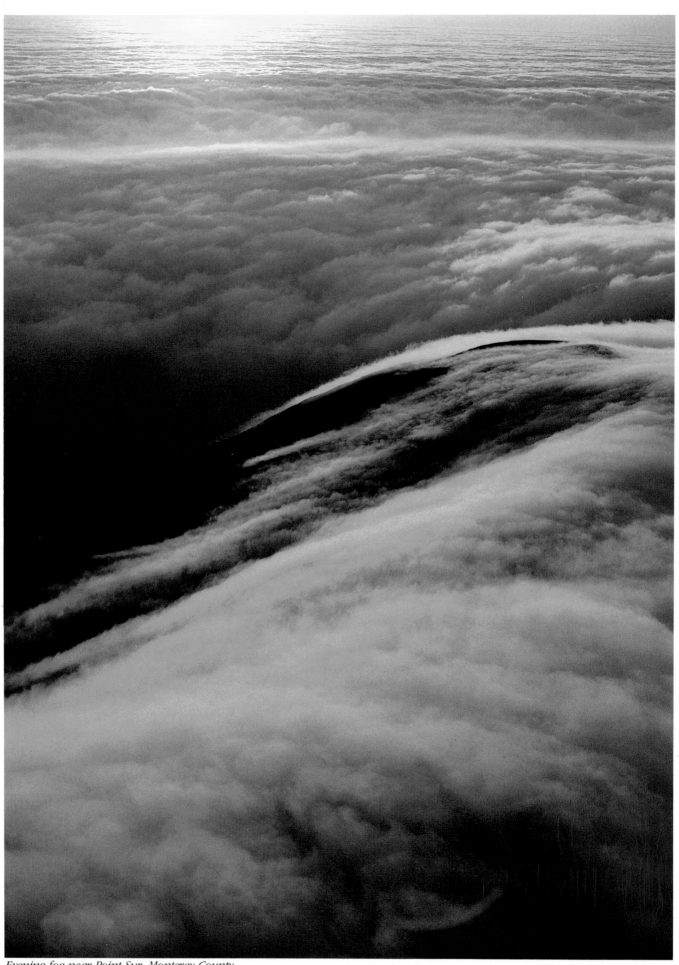

Evening fog near Point Sur, Monterey County

T H A N K S . . . .

At the end of 1977 the rains finally returned to California. There had been a long, devastating drought, months of cloudless skies. The ground was dry and cracking, reservoirs were low or empty. The earth was parched, every living thing was hued in brown.

When the rains came again the portions were generous. Seeds, long dormant, sprouted with fresh growth. Wilted plants straightened and held their limbs upward as before. The lakes filled, the streams ran. The hills and the valleys and the plains turned green once more.

In the spring of 1978, Jon Carroll, then editor of *New West*, telephoned. He knew my obsession with aerial photography and flight, and he wanted a portrait from the air of California after the drought. When the photos appeared in the July 31st issue, he wrote, "It was the most bountiful, overwhelming spring within living memory." And so it was. It was also the spring in which the idea for this book was born. For our journey throughout California often took us along the coast, introduced us to vistas of normally unseen beauty, gave us a greater sense of the over-changing relationship between land and water — dimensions mostly invisible from the more limited vantage point on the ground.

So the acknowledgements begin with special thanks to Jon and to *New West*. Then to book expert Dick Schuettge who warmed to the idea immediately and continued his enthusiasm for the project even as mine temporarily waned. As did Leslie Patrick, friend and counselor, who also turned the heat up whenever I moved the book to the back burner. In a flash John Burks put together a team of professional scribes who turned ideas and conversations into meaningful text; John's own introductions and impeccable editing assured a quality flow of words.

Because they recognized a good deal, Susan Resendez, Philip Carville, Susan Wolman and Steven Guggenheim gave at the office. Their commitment and support is greatly appreciated, and I'm glad they're aboard.

Thanks to Fran Bolei, Susan Greenburg and Dolores Coleman for turning sounds on tape into words on pages. Thanks to Michael Goodwin, Tom Johnson and Dick Thompson for finding and talking to our coastal heroes. These folks — interviewers and interviewees — made all the difference.

My hand to Phil Carroll and Georgia Gillfillan, and to Janet Hansen. Working inhuman hours while the rest of the world rested or played, they took the raw material — photos and words — and created a book, a beautiful book, a lovely book, a special book.

Of course you can't make aerial photos without an airplane. So thanks to Vindar of Novato for the planes and instructors, and for running a tight ship. And to Garvin Brown for the wherewithal to purchase the cherry Cessna 172 when it was needed.

It's possible — but not always prudent — to fly and photograph at the same time. Especially around populated areas where other planes cruise by with some regularity. So, for the most part, these photographs were taken from one side, through an open window, while a bona fide pilot flew the plane from the other side. No one individual had the time to accompany me on all flights, but many were generous. Cyd Fougner, above all. Back in the early days we would come in high over the "target area" for a panoramic shot. Then Cyd would lower the nose above a small cameo on the ground that particularly fascinated me and down we'd come, quickly and accurately, circling for the best angle. Cyd had a knack for holding the plane in the proper attitude: wing just high enough, wheel just low enough, the strut ahead and just out of sight. She became intuitive and occasionally knew before I where the lens would come to rest. Cyd also happened to be my flight instructor; from her I learned the important fine points (and some of the fun points) of flying. We shared some great photo missions before she was hired as a flight engineer on a Boeing jet for Western Airlines.

Fred Padula flew for the first *New West* series. Fred is also a photographer; he's an excellent pilot and one of the partners of the small Cessna in which we both learned to fly. Jim Sugar, another pilot/photographer, and with whom I now share the 172, not only flew for me, but countered my natural indolence with an insistence we stay in the air even after the sun dropped below the horizon. The result was, of course, some stunningly beautiful colors peculiar to dusk aloft. George Hall, with whom I collaborated on both editions of the *Blimp Book*, took the controls on more than one occasion, as did author/pilot/motorcyclist Steven L. Thompson. Peter Garrison, the Echo Park genius of *Melmoth* fame and my partner on *Homebuilt Airplanes*, did a stint or two in the skies over Southern California, and in spirit at least, George Larson often shared the cockpit. To this lady and to these gentlemen my gratitude and appreciation for accompanying me into the third dimension.

Aerial photography is easier than it sounds but more difficult than it looks. Some technical adjustments have to be made: for example, the ASA rating must be doubled to avoid overexposing the film. Shutter speeds should be kept at 1/250th or above whenever possible; long lens problems are also magnified by the motion and vibration of the aircraft. And at 90 miles an hour there is very little time to quietly compose and frame each shot. Rather, a second sense must be developed that mentally compares the rate of turn to the ever changing image, anticipating the right moment to release the shutter just before it actually appears in the finder.

To my mind the best pictures are made when the shadows are long and the light is rich and warm, usually in the early morning or late afternoon. Unstable weather results in interesting photos. Rainclouds are more graphically exciting than blue sky, and as a bonus they give the sun a secondary palette, above the horizon.

The pictures were made with a Nikon FE on Kodachrome 64 film. There were six lenses in the bag: 28mm, 35mm, 50mm, 85mm, 180mm and an 80-200 zoom, all Nikkor. Occasionally I would add a polarizer if the angle to the sun was right and the clouds were cooperative. It was helpful to have the motor drive, not because I like to squeeze off five frames a second, but because I could keep my eye at the viewer and watch the image move by, rather than having to pull the camera away each time to wind the shutter and advance the film. All photography was done from a Cessna 172; it's a delightfully stable airplane with windows that open and wings above and a willingness to fly gentle at relatively slow speeds.

Hanging out above the coast has been a marvelous experience. I'm appreciative to all my friends for the multifaceted collaboration, and I'm happy we shared the process of building this book. I sincerely hope each feels the result was worth the effort. I certainly do. □

Baron Wolman
Mill Valley, 1981

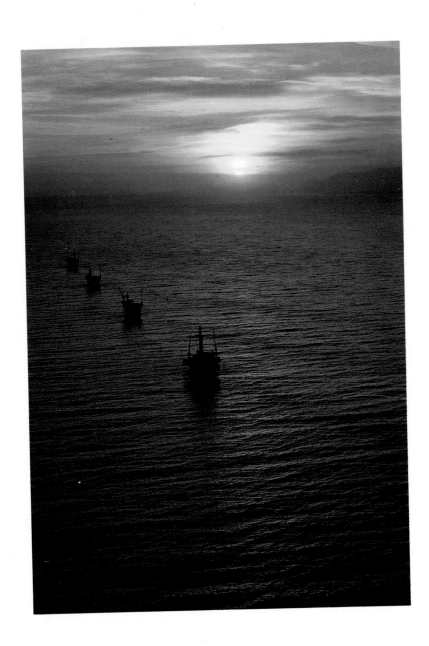